The Sky Isn't Visible from Here

The Sky Isn't Visible from Here

by Felicia C. Sullivan

ALGONQUIN BOOKS OF CHAPEL HILL 2008

Published by
Algonquin Books of Chapel Hill
Post Office Box 2225
Chapel Hill, North Carolina 27515-2225

a division of
Workman Publishing
225 Varick Street
New York, New York 10014

This is a true story. However, names and identifying details have been changed and some characters have been combined. Dialogue has been re-created and certain events have been presented out of order. To write this book, I have relied on memories, which are subjective, and in some cases I've relied on what my mother told me.

Library of Congress Cataloging-in-Publication Data
Sullivan, Felicia C.
    The sky isn't visible from here / by Felicia C. Sullivan. — 1st ed.
      p. cm.
    ISBN-13: 978-1-56512-515-5
    1. Sullivan, Felicia C. 2. Drug addicts — New York (State) — New
York — Biography. 3. Adult children of drug addicts — New York
(State) — New York — Biography. 4. Cocaine abuse — New York (State) —
New York. 5. Adult child sexual abuse victims — New York (State) — New
York — Biography. I. Title.
HV5805.S85A3 2007
362.76092 — dc22
    [B]   2006101290

10 9 8 7 6 5 4 3 2 1
First Edition

For Fergus

Contents

Prologue

IN THE SPRING OF 1997, a few weeks before my college graduation, my mother disappeared. Over the years, I had grown used to her leaving: a four-day cocaine binge; a wedding at City Hall to which I was not invited; the month she locked herself behind her bedroom door and emerged only to buy cigarettes. I'd spent the greater part of my life feeling abandoned by my mother. Yet she'd always return — blazing into the kitchen to cook up a holiday feast for ten when the table was set for only three or creeping past me at dawn, red-eyed and sullen, back from her drug dealer on Brooklyn's Ninth Avenue.

On the morning of my graduation, though, dressed in a black gown, I walked up the promenade to receive my diploma, scanning the audience. My mother's face didn't appear among the proud, applauding parents. I knew then that I'd never see her again. Her deserting me for yet another man (this one had tried to strangle her) marked her death for me. This time I cut *her* out of *my* life: I collected photographs, birthday cards—anything that would remind me of her—and sealed them in a box along with a painful past to which I swore I'd never return.

I had been in perpetual chrysalis for most of my life, but during college I'd become an expert at transformation. I turned into a walking J.Crew catalog: preened, preppy, and audaciously New England. Like a barnacle, I clung desperately to my affluent Waspy friends, most of them blonds who owned platinum Rolex watches that cost more than used cars. Unbeknownst to them, they were my teachers on all matters of etiquette and style. I mimicked their expressions and copied their wardrobes. I hoarded books on place settings, practicing a proper table on top of my bed. And I never let down my hair. Literally. I have curly hair—the kinky, unruly kind—but I wore it ironed straight. The difference between wearing my hair straight or curly was the difference between life and death.

Now, I took the invention of myself a step further. When I began graduate school, I resolved to no longer be the child who took her mother to the hospital when her body convulsed from all the drugs. Instead I became a young woman who hailed from Long Island with a mother who'd quietly passed away and a father who bred horses. This was all partially true. When I was a teenager my mother and I moved out of Brooklyn and into a four-room apartment on the South Shore of Long Island that we shared with Gus, my mother's fiancé, who to this day I call my father. Every day at dawn, Gus drove out to Brookville to break yearlings and raise thoroughbred horses.

As a graduate student I became guarded about my past and my previous life, never mentioning the summer my mother and I survived on bags of potatoes and butter, or the ever burgeoning piles of empty Bacardi bottles, or the images of my mother, in a violent rage, ripping my writing to shreds. I didn't tell anyone that Jade, the woman my mother left me with when I was little who drank countless tumblers of vodka lemonade, was out cold when her teenage son came home one night, boom box on his shoulder, wanting to know what I looked like on the inside. My mother bludgeoned Jade's son with Jade's own skillet, broke his nose in two places, and cracked his jaw. Afterward, my mother insisted this never happened. Like everything else—a broken arm, my mother sleeping with men for money and drugs while I lay on the floor next to her bed—all these memories, she was adamant, were my imagination.

These memories were now locked in a room to which I permitted no entry.

Sometimes, though, my past would come back to me in flashes, horrific storms, and I would shudder and say aloud, *That person, that life, is not you.* And, of course, there were other ways to forget: I'd had my first blackout from alcohol at seventeen and, at twenty-four, my first from cocaine.

Still, I was proud of my creation: a college graduate, a master's candidate, a woman who worked in the most prestigious investment banks, read Sartre and Woolf, and owned a collection of expensive handbags and shoes. Eventually, however, the weight of these two lives—one perfectly assembled on paper and another lived in incessant fear of being found out—grew too difficult to bear. There were near heart attacks in taxicabs, nosebleeds at work, a leave of absence from graduate school, a strained relationship with Gus, and friends who avoided my phone calls.

And then there was my mother—whom I never truly mourned —ghosting my waking and sleeping hours. I began to wonder if I'd been trying to drink and snort my way back to her, a woman who loved her alcohol and drugs too.

THESE ARE THE THINGS I know about my mother: she was a junkie, a liar, a thief, a woman who made the very best golden-fried chicken cutlets, who tried to protect me from the world and all the people in it, a mother who didn't know how to be a mother. And she is also the woman who broke my heart. The last time we spoke I remember telling her, *You make it impossible for me to love you.* I thought then that loving my mother was killing me, but now I know *I* was killing me.

I decided it was time to come clean. I told my friends that my mother did not quietly pass away. There was no funeral, no spadefuls of earth. I told them that I hadn't seen my mother in a decade. I knew nothing of her now—where she lived, if she lived at all. With trepidation, my friends asked, *So your mother didn't die?*

Define die, I said. It's possible that she's dead, but I don't know.

My friends were surprised to learn that Gus, the man they'd come to know as my father, wasn't my birth father. They asked after my real father. When I was young, my aunt told me that my mother banished him: since he had left her, hurt her, there was no way he would know his daughter. *That's what happens,* my mother had said, *when you break my fucking heart.* My freshman year of college, my mother, angry, told me that I had been the product of a rape, but another time she claimed that my father was Peruvian, and then there was that time she said he was American Indian and they had planned to get married at an Indian reservation out West. With my mother you never knew what to believe.

Shamefully, I admitted to my friends that I'd done coke in their houses, in their bathrooms, off their bedroom dressers, that I'd stolen pills out of bathroom cabinets, wine from their kitchens. They wondered, *How did we not know?* But these are the same people who thought my hair was straight and laughed when I insisted that I was really shy, scared of new people, that podiums frighten me, that I used to stutter. It was exhausting working a room, smiling those happy-meal smiles. They found this hard to believe, *Look at that reading series you curated, that journal you publish, all us friends you've acquired. You are the human telephone book. You,* they insisted, *are the opposite of shy.* But it was just that I'd always thought it was my job to make sure everyone else was happy.

IT'S BEEN FIVE YEARS since my last line of cocaine. I've kept friends and made many new ones since then, friends of many hues: red, black, brown, blond (to be fair). And my new best friend, well, everything about her is loud, from her gum chewing to her infectious laugh, but I love her in ways I couldn't have ever imagined. Last year we took a trip to see her family in Taiwan, and I remember emerging from the showers at a public pool, my curly, coarse hair dripping wet. And it took everything in me not to cry when she came up behind me, touched my hair, and said, *You're beautiful.*

The Sky Isn't Visible from Here

Part One

Fighting Shoes

IN BROOKLYN, MY MOTHER and I lived with a man named Avram who taught me two sentences in Hebrew: *I love you* and *I need five hundred dollars.* His body was covered in hair as thick as wool, but his skin was slick, smoothed with baby oil. He never left the house without Afrin nasal spray and toothpicks. Avi drove a station wagon with buckets of paint, turpentine, and brushes cluttering the backseat. On the way to school he always warned, "Whatever you do in the dark comes out in the light," as if he knew a secret of mine that he would ferret out. But I was ten then; I read Judy Blume and wore mismatched socks. I'd already learned how to keep my secrets hidden away, safe.

FELICIA C. SULLIVAN

Avram was a man who spoke little, so whenever he spoke, you listened. I wonder how it was that he introduced my mother to cocaine: whether there were words at all or if it was simply a pouch of white in his moist palm and a promise of omnipotence. They went from smoking joints while watching *Dynasty* and passing commentary on Sammie Jo or the silliness of shoulder pads—it was 1985, but Avi and my mother still donned bell-bottoms and paisley, trying to remain in the seventies, that wild-child decade, for as long as they could—to cutting up lines of cocaine. Later, I'd hear my mother crying out *"Avi!"* their heads smashing up against the headboard. My walls shook.

I imagined them at Brighton Beach, lapping up fat lines with cut straws. They were like any other couple on the beach, drinking malt liquor until they were a little drunk. But then they drank some more. They passed a roach between their fingers, taking tokes. In broad daylight, they dabbed seawater under their noses, inhaling any remnants of coke. They hoarded their highs. I pictured them digging their heels deep into the soggy sand, feeling the gravel between their toes. My mother would marvel at the hot sun dipping into the waves, which had turned black. The water beckoned, but she would inch her body up the shoreline because she felt both comforted by and frightened of the ocean. She would smile then, but only slightly, ashamed of her teeth, which were yellowed and fanged. My mother vehemently avoided the dentist and rarely let anyone see her teeth. To the world she was fair and sexy. While my mother's and Avi's cheeks flushed and their necks turned pink, I would be home alone, sitting on the grates of the

4

fire escape, watching the black squirrels desperately scavenge for food in the trees, waiting for her and Avi to come home.

MY MOTHER OWNED a pair of dark red Pumas with dirty white laces. Bits of rubber had frayed from the sides; the soles were so worn that the cotton from her slouchy socks poked through. Whenever she squeezed her feet into the sneakers, one, then the other, she would yank on the laces, hard, and double knot them, rabbit style. She usually put them on when she was going to fight someone, but often she wore them to work because they were comfortable, unlike her work shoes, which pinched her feet. You never knew if she was on her way to work or to a brawl. She called the Pumas her shit kickers.

If provoked, she would pounce on anyone, all five foot two of her, and slam her fists into their face, blinding them with punches. If ever I were teased at school, pushed or picked on, braids tugged, I kept it secret. Living on perpetual tiptoe, I learned not to rouse her.

Dressed in her hideous pinstripe waitress uniform, she walked home early from work one day, past my schoolyard, and waved at me, her little green order pad nestled in her belt. I couldn't tell if she came by to greet me or to sniff out a scuffle. In the schoolyard, Tamika strutted toward me, her thick braids slapping her chin, the kinky ends scratching her cheeks. I clutched at my black velvet skirt, pouffed out by layers of cheap organza beneath, the ribbons of my white ruffled blouse sticking to my sweaty skin. It was class picture day for us fifth graders, and my mother had braided my coarse, curly hair into two fat pigtails and tied them with red ribbons to match the ones on my blouse. I looked like an idiot.

Tamika pointed at me and laughed. "Silly *bambina blanca!*" she said. She poked a chubby finger into my rib cage and my legs buckled. Her friends surrounded me in a half circle, snorting. Elsa giggled. Raquel sneered. Soft squeals rose from my throat. I choked them down quickly. My mother, who was standing at the curb smoking a Kent 100, stomped up in the Pumas.

"We got a problem here?" she asked, hands planted firmly on her hips, cigarette gripped at the corner of her mouth. Her breathing was easy, calm. My mother was fearless; if you'd put a gun to her head, her pulse wouldn't have broken seventy. She waited patiently for Tamika to respond. She would wait all day if she had to; pull up a chair, smoke through her pack, buy another. Because she lived for this drama: making people squirm, breaking them down. And then she gave Tamika the *look,* brows knitted, pupils constricted—her glare pulverized you, sucked the air from inside out. Tamika shivered. I felt very small.

Tamika dragged the sole of her sneaker from one side to the other as if she were drawing an invisible line between herself and my mother. My mother sucked her teeth. Spitting the cigarette out, she repeated, "You got a problem?" The cigarette lay on the ground, burning to the filter.

"Ain't no problem here," Tamika said. Her crew eased back, their feet making careful steps.

When my mother turned to me, her face softened. She retied the ribbons on my braids, adjusted my skirt. Her long fingernails picked at bits of fuzz on my blouse, and with one sweep she wiped off any traces of lint. Once my mother turned her head, sneakers skidded on the ground as the girls sprinted toward the school entrance door, which they flung open. I pulled away and lowered my head. I could have died. I could have melted into the asphalt in shame. And nothing would be left but my velvet skirt, polyester blouse, and scarlet ribbons.

After that day, my mother made it her routine to pass by on her lunch hour and wave. Her hair was always pulled back into a tight braid, her skin stretched tight, as if it were plastered against her face. With a free hand, she smoothed her scalp, and all the flyaway strands obeyed and buried themselves beneath the mountain of rubber bands that held her hair in place. Every morning she lathered Maybelline Tawny Beige foundation into her skin, creating a tan mask — dark tan, she could be Dominican; lighter tan, she could be Puerto Rican — even though everyone in the neighborhood knew we were white people blending in. Her transformation was dramatic: She'd enter the bathroom Irish and fair, thick coats of blue mascara and peach lipstick would follow the foundation, and when she left for work her skin would appear several shades darker. Only her neck betrayed her paleness. Years ago, when she dated black men, she lathered on the make-up even darker and spoke with a Spanish accent. When she slept with white men, she was Rosina Sullivan, the pasty white girl.

Kids became scared of friendship with me. One wrong word, a slight nudge on my shoulder, a sly joke, and my mother would come running in her red Pumas. Palming each other's backs, the

Dominican girls huddled in a tight circle, *"Todos sabes acerca de tu mamá."* Black girls tried to act tough, shoulders erect, heads held high, but they hushed in my presence. Everyone in Boro Park knew about my mother; she awed them because she was beautiful and dangerous. She appeared never to sleep, as if she even rested with one eye open. She was nothing like the other mothers, who held court on stoops, arms folded in, talking about everything and nothing.

"I CAN'T BREATHE," my mother said one Saturday night, shaking me back and forth in my twin bed. My Glo Worm night-light was hot and burned dimly in the room. I dreaded the weekends because they were always her worst time. Free from the obligations of waitressing—of waking at five in the morning, of pressing her uniform and wiping her sneakers clean—she was free to play, to go out dancing, linger at the beach, or worse, spend nights out with Avi, nights that always ended up with them laughing and snorting coke until dawn.

Sitting on the edge of my bed now, she pulled my sheet down with the weight of her body, which had whittled down to bone. I rubbed my eyes and grabbed my glasses from the nightstand. The room smelled of her perfume, Love's Baby Soft, a mixture of sweet powder and vanilla musk.

I sat up and said, "You want me to call a cab?"

"Yeah," she whispered, her breath straining as if it would be her last.

I wasn't fooled. She wasn't dying. This scene had played out before. I would sit in the cab in silence while she panted. We would enter the hospital, me clutching her shirt, her recoiling in disgust, "You'll wrinkle my shirt!" I would wait for her in the dingy waiting room, a putrid brown film coating the walls like wallpaper, lime green and orange plastic oval chairs lumpy with chewing gum. Passing time by watching the clock's hands, I knew it might be hours before her return. Later I would hear the familiar stomp in the hall, and there she would be, appearing confident, as if nothing had happened.

Sometimes she dropped the powder-blue pamphlets in the trash can outside the hospital; other times she left them on the floor in the back of the cab. I snatched one once and it opened like an accordion. Facing Your Addiction, it read. I crumpled it into a tight ball, surprised by how neatly it fit in my hand.

And here we were tonight, back to where we always started, me calling the car service to Maimonides Hospital and her convinced that this trip would be her last. As I slid out of the two layers of blankets, all my stuffed animals fell to the floor in a collective *thump*. My mother eased her frame into the imprint I had made in the bed and then stared at the wall.

"I'll call the cab," I said.

"Hurry," she said, placing her hand on her chest. The other hand held a cigarette, which she drew slowly to her lips. Blood trickled from her left nostril. She sniffed it back.

I ran back into the room and scooped up a book from my nightstand. Waiting-room material.

Before I even said the address: "We know where you live, kid."

The dispatcher's voice was throaty, sympathetic. On my tiptoes, I reached high to place the receiver back into the cradle. I stood in the darkness of the kitchen, my feet cold against the linoleum squares.

"Did you call?" She was in the living room now; her voice had grown louder. I looked at the door, at the various locks, chains, and deadbolts, and I wanted to run.

"I called," I said.

"What?" she hollered, dragging her feet across the carpet, making her way into the kitchen.

"You have to put your shoes on," I said. She had on her pink slippers, the ones with the pebbled white soles. I powered past, grabbed her shoes, and kneeled. My eyes could barely focus on the tattered laces; my lids kept easing down like a silk curtain dropping. I concentrated on tying a double knot. If I could just get this one knot. If I could just do this.

"Get the Pumas," she said, coughing. Her body was volcanic. Under her breath, she kept saying, "Damn you, Avi." The cigarette slipped from her fingers onto the kitchen floor. From the street, a car horn beeped twice, waited a few minutes, beeped again. I threw my coat over my Strawberry Shortcake pajamas and helped my mother down the four flights of stairs. We took it slow and my mother was impatient. "Jesus, Lisa, can you move any slower? I could be dying here." She called me Lisa because Avi couldn't pronounce my name and they decided it was easier than Felicia. Lately she used my given name only when she was angry or in public. She leaned into me, even her skeletal weight becoming hard to bear. Still she crushed cockroaches all the way down. I gripped the plastic bag with the Pumas. My knuckles turned white when she proudly yelled, "I got seven of the fuckers!"

Avi was gone, away on another one of his trips to Atlantic City, playing blackjack and roulette with the hope of scoring big. The kind of score that buys you a month's supply, keeps away the men who call and ask about the money you owe, when and how will you pay it. And I wondered about what kind of boy Avram had been. What kind of boy grows into a man who offers up cocaine like fairy dust, sprinkles it everywhere my mother walks, and then leaves for weeks at a time?

"Maimonides Hospital, right?" the driver asked, staring at me in the mirror.

"Is there anywhere else?" I answered, sliding into the leather seat.

A FEW WEEKS BACK, I had walked the seven blocks from school to the shabby diner on Thirteenth Avenue where my mother worked. The windows were smudged and dirty from fingerprints and the grease that rose from the grill. The menu, taped on from the inside, was filthy. Butter had soaked through the "Specials" and grape jelly was smeared over the "Meat" entrees.

My mother stood behind the counter, refilling ketchup bottles. She'd taken all the half-empty ones and turned one bottle upside down so that the mouths met, executing this task with such precision that she didn't allow a drop of the paste to spurt out of the bottle and stain the counter. When she saw me, she traipsed over to the soda fountain and filled a tall glass with ice and Coca-Cola. She placed it in front of me as I climbed onto the stool, my hands pressing the leather seat for leverage.

She leaned her elbows on the counter and drummed her fingers on her chin. "Grilled cheese or blueberry muffin?"

"Muffin, of course," I said. Within moments, my mother slid a steaming mushroom-shape mass before me. I picked at the crust on the edges, circling the muffin's top, breaking off bits of bread and berry, then nibbling down to the minor scraps. A man stared at me, his fleshy pink lips curved into a smile.

"Got a system there with that muffin, kid?"

And then suddenly my mother was screaming. The whole of the diner was paralyzed, which is not to say that mouths paused in midbite or feet froze in a shuffle, but the customers set their forks down and voices fell to a hushed murmur. They stared. She was her own circus attraction. All the muscles in her face tightened. Blue veins punched through the sides of her neck. Spit flew in the air.

"You don't think I hear what the fuck you're saying?" she shouted. She marched out from behind the counter toward a table where two men were seated. Both wore baseball caps stained with oil and soot. They clutched their spoons, frightened. Hands on her hips, she spat in the face of the thinner man in a Camel cap.

The other waitress begged, "Rosie, your *kid*!"

My mother glared at her, then turned back to the man. "You got something to say about me? You want to say it to my face?"

The other man's fingers clutched a strip of bacon, his mouth buried in a white beard. "Moving around the tables kinda fast is all we we're saying."

"A little too awake," the other timidly added. "A little too much of the powder." He tapped his nose.

The bearded man slouched back in his seat. "You should be ashamed, with your kid here and all. Shit, Rosie, everyone knows what you're doing."

He chuckled and my mother laughed with him. She tilted her head so far back I thought it would snap. I didn't know if I should run or stay put. I just wanted the men to go away, for her to walk over and refill my soda. Didn't they know not to provoke her?

The restaurant was reduced to a collection of inverted faces, of nudging and whispering as her laughter snowballed. From the kitchen, the cook journeyed toward her, but before he could reach her, before he could hold her back, she grabbed the bearded man's plate and smashed it over his head. Yolk slid down his face as he jumped out of the booth, knocking down his Coke. He slipped on the soda and collapsed on the floor. My mother smiled and turned to me.

"I'll see you at home," she said, waving me away.

THE YELLOW CRACKS in the ceiling had spread since the last time I'd sat in this hospital waiting for my mother. The loudspeaker dangled from a thin black ceiling wire. People whispered, played spades, and fiddled with their radios until they were hailed to the white rooms behind the plaid curtains. Beside me, a small boy shifted from side to side, his honey skin luminous in the false overhead lights. We were watching *Benny Hill* on a television that hung, like the loudspeaker, from the ceiling. The boy wore white Pampers and stunk of urine.

My grip tightened around the handles of the plastic bag that held the Pumas. I picked at the plastic, tearing off slivers and dropping them to the ground like snowflakes. Furious with my mother, I shredded the plastic until the shoes tumbled to the floor, barely making a sound when they hit, one then the other.

A young woman with fluid dark hair pulled back in a loose ponytail clutched a clipboard. The nurses behind the station laughed. I heard static from their radio. I leaned over my chair, picked the Pumas off the floor, and held them to my nose, breathing in. They smelled like my mother, the perfume and sweat from her beige nylons.

This was how it always felt, waiting for my mother.

Of My Kind

MANHATTAN 2001

OVER DINNER MY FRIEND Merritt tells me, "We're warriors, look how far we've come." We clink glasses. Later Merritt will snort crushed horse tranquilizers and Vicodin like dime-store candy and I will do thick lines. But now, in this restaurant, she plays the role of a successful hedge-fund manager and I of a project manager at a media company that sells cable, high-speed internet service, and over two hundred TV channels I'm not sure anyone needs. Merritt cackles when she laughs, and lives her life as if these are the last days of disco. She is blond, like all the friends I keep. We are twenty-five, invincible. We ease into a second bottle of wine.

Glass tips. Wine spills. "Come, drink," it calls. "Have another."

"Do you hear me?" she says, "We're fucking warriors, *survivors*."

"Warriors and survivors are two different things," I say.

"You're a dictionary now?"

I tell Merritt that tomorrow I have an appointment, a consultation to sell my eggs. To cover credit-card debt, rent for the apartment in Little Italy, I say, but my friend knows better. Merritt knows how much cocaine eight thousand dollars could buy. I describe the cryptic phone calls from the clinic — it's all very covert — the forms I've filled in, and the fact that I've leveraged myself much like a dirty junk bond; I'm worth more because of my Ivy League pedigree.

"But you're on leave from Columbia," Merritt says.

"They don't need the details," I say.

"They'll test you."

"I don't plan on failing," I say. I remind Merritt how I soared through my company's drug test. I cleaned myself up for a week, practically overdosing on vitamins and green tea.

"When does your trip back to sobriety begin?"

"Tomorrow," I say. Around me the air thickens; a sedative cloud forms and everything is dulled. The volume in the restaurant turns down low. Voices thin to a singular sustained drone. People move in slow motion. But the lights, they're still too bright and glaring. I notice my empty glass.

"Well, then," Merritt says, glancing at the bathroom, "let's do you a proper bon voyage."

• • •

LATER THAT NIGHT I gnaw at my pillow, coil the sheets to a double helix around my ankles. I can't wake up. In my dream there are children everywhere and my mother and I are the only adults among them. We are in the country this time, and they run through fresh-cut fields. There is no sound here, but there are black squirrels, rabbits, possibly a fox. Two freckled, pale-haired, peach-skinned children appear to me in microscopic detail. Their clothes are the color of sky—they wear blue pantaloons and white sailor caps. They're beautiful and clean in a way that disturbs me. These are children who are children. Nothing about them resembles my mother or me or our somber landscape of blacks and grays; they must take after the father they're privileged to know. They collect around my mother's knees, which are tan and smooth. She never used to shave. When did she start shaving? I can't see her face; daylight shields her from me. The children tug at my mother's arms, their faces scrunched up, eyes narrowing into slits as if they've been staring at the sun for longer than they should. They are happier than I've ever been because my mother loves them. The children are her property. They call her mommy, and then they point at me and say, "Why does that lady look just like you?" My mother's feet move in reverse. The children follow her. They always do.

My grinding teeth wake me.

IN THE WAITING ROOM I fill out more forms. Parenting magazines are spread out on the coffee table, the glossy ones that show blue-eyed infants on the cover, feet dangling, wide smiles exposing chickpea teeth. I've called in sick to work, which is a lie but not entirely untrue, because I feel sick. The air conditioner's frigid gusts are more aggravating than refreshing. My stomach turns. In this large room, I'm the only one waiting. I'm good at this, I think, the waiting. Ever since I was ten, I've sat alone in hospitals while doctors dispensed tranquilizers to my mother, tried to calm her down because she loved her cocaine and she kept doing too much of it.

An hour later I sit in another carpeted, air-conditioned office, pimping myself out to a stranger. Degrees from NYU, Johns Hopkins, and Hunter hang on the walls. I say all the right things. I glance at the intake coordinator in her flimsy acrylic dress, matching blazer with pilled sleeves, worn leather pumps, the eyeglasses too big for her face, and then up at the framed degrees, and I wonder whether she really earned them. The intake coordinator goes on about how rare it is to meet a candidate who is both creative and pragmatic. Here is my work history in order: Chase, Morgan, a now-defunct dot-com, and currently a media company. Eight years playing the clarinet, two years of operating a private online business that I incorporated—I get the sense that this woman might skip all the tests and adopt me herself. Fidgety, I continue to speak in exclamation points.

We schedule a follow-up appointment for the physical and psychological evaluation. Before I leave, she briefly confirms some basic health-related questions. I deliver her a potential egg donor in perfect health who drinks one, maybe two, glasses of wine a week and has never experimented with drugs.

"Not even marijuana?" she asks. "Maybe in college? Perhaps with friends on the weekend?"

I laugh and say, "Look at me. When would I have the time?"

TONIGHT SHE'S NAKED, swathed in my overwashed blue cotton baby blanket with the matching blue satin trim. I was never a child who took to pink. My mother lies in my bathroom sink, arms stretched wide, calling out to me. The room smells of bleach and cigarette smoke. She's chalk white save for black pearl eyes and the thatch of hair below her navel. The dream begins this way—I'm the one in control—and ends differently.

Her voice is garbled, all baby talk and drooling coos, when I cut in. "Speak up," I say, tapping my watch. "I don't have all night."

Her lips press together hard, in a way that makes me tense. Her face might splinter, erode like paint chipping or peeling, like walls collapsing inward. I see Avi. I see rolled-up hundred-dollar bills and Afrin nose spray. I remember cutting my foot on glass in Atlantic City; Avi licked the wound clean. Wrapping his wife beater under my foot, he said, "You don't need alcohol. You don't need that kind of pain." Inside the casino, my mother made a killing at the slots.

"You probably thought you were stronger. I can't say that I blame you. Watching Marisol overdose, I thought I was, too. But it sneaks up on you, it does," my mother says, still in the sink. "How could I have possibly helped you?"

"Who said I need you? Who said I ever needed you?" I say.

"You poor girl, you thought I'd come back and save you," she says. Her legs sprout hair and dangle off the sink's edge. She surveys my bathroom, the expensive shower curtain, the plush matching bath mat, pomades and salts that smell of sandalwood and lavender. She eyes my loofah, my French conditioner, the obsessively bleached-clean tub and floors. "I'll say one thing, you keep a house better than I ever could. Tell me, Lisa, do you pay someone to clean all this?" She reconsiders. "No, that wouldn't be you. You'd get down on your knees. Use your hands. You're that kind."

"I'm not your kind," I say.

Shaking her head, she says, "Who else's would you be?"

I claw my arms, try to wake up, but I'm still here, in the dream, trapped with my mother.

I'M NOT GOOD around needles. I turn away when a nurse presses one into my arm, draws two tubes of blood. They will test for HIV, glucose levels; they will ascertain cell counts, look for abnormalities: anemia, diabetes, a possible heart condition. The nurse tells me that I have better veins in my hands than in my arms.

"I'll keep that in mind," I say.

Next is the urine sample—routine, of course—which will determine whether I'm drug free. Over the past week I've done everything short of ingesting Pine Sol to cleanse my system.

"Your counselor will have the results next week," the nurse says, labeling the tubes and cup with my name in her neat penmanship. She tosses her plastic gloves into a waste bin. The radio dial is set to the easy-listening station.

I ride another elevator to another floor, where I meet a psychologist. Anne is older than any counselors I have known, possibly in her late fifties, and I immediately decide that I do not like her. She wears a wool crepe pantsuit and Ferragamo flats. Her face is doughy, a double-ply cashmere. She might possibly be wearing my perfume, Angel, but it is sweeter off her skin; it fills the room, displacing me. And I've never seen anyone past the age of thirty with a French manicure. I loathe her. You are not my mother, I think. You are not young.

Anne asks me if I've ever been in therapy.

"Hasn't everyone? I think if you live in New York and you *don't* have a therapist something's wrong with you," I say.

"So you're currently seeing someone?"

I think of my therapist, Ellen, and her phone calls that I've neglected to return. I tried to convince her that I was better, that I no longer needed her, and she reluctantly let me go. "I'm concerned, Felicia, I don't feel our work is done," she said. For eight months I'd been lying my way through therapy, anyway. Playing the role of the recovered addict who now spends her weekends in various yoga poses or making mousses and apple crumbles instead of curled up under dirty sheets, all the blinds pulled down, drapes closed, no light permitted, surviving on a bottle of water at the foot of the bed, a half-empty bottle of Xanax under my pillow. "I'm fine," I said to Ellen, handing her my final check, "so fine, don't I look fine?" As I left her office, Ellen sighed and said, "With you, sometimes I don't know."

"I was seeing someone, but I don't see her anymore," I say.

Anne nods. I grip the arm of the leather chair.

"For a long time I was angry with my mother."

"And now?" Anne asks.

"My mother disappeared five years ago."

"What do you mean by disappeared?" Anne asks.

"One day she called a taxi. It waited outside for her. She took the TV, my albums, and her leather jackets. She opened our front door, left it open, got in the taxi, closed that door, and she left. I would tell you more, but I wasn't there. I was in Chicago. My father called me."

"Are you still angry?"

"It was five years ago," I say. "I don't have time to be angry. I don't have time to think about why my mother left us for a man who tried to strangle her."

"Has she tried to contact you?"

I'm quiet. I rip a hangnail. I bleed. I remember the leaving. I remember sitting on the floor surrounded by sponges and Ajax and crying. It was the summer before my senior year of college. I scrubbed our apartment walls, buried her cat that died of distemper (the one thing she did love but forgot to take); I packed the whole of our lives into cardboard boxes, moved my father, Gus, and me to another apartment. Gus isn't my real father but he's the only father I've ever known. I don't tell the counselor that. I remember our couch not fitting through the door. The cardboard boxes that gave way and me screaming at all the books and dishes flying down the stairs. That day was a photograph I wanted to shred.

"Felicia?"

"My senior year in college she called me from her neighbor's pay phone a few weeks before graduation. She was living in a one-room apartment, eating bread. The man she had left us for had tried to strangle her. She'd lost the feeling in her hands, she said." Could I come save her? Could I bring her back home? Couldn't Gus and I forgive her for leaving? Because what she'd done, her leaving, wasn't so terrible.

"I told her I was done, that I couldn't take it anymore," I say.

"And what did she say?" Anne asks.

"'*Fuck you.*' Then she hung up."

"Was that the last time you heard from your mother?"

"She conned her neighbor into telling me she died. I called Gus, crying, but he didn't buy the story. I know that woman, he said, and drove out to her one-room apartment in New Hyde Park. He saw her holding hands with the man who had tried to kill her just the week before. Apparently she wanted me to think she died. It worked. She's dead to me."

Like everyone else who's heard the story, Anne asks, "Have you tried to find her?"

I sigh. I've grown used to these questions. Sometimes people ask, Would I find her if I could, don't I want to find her, doesn't she want to be found and forgiven? As if it's up to me alone to find her. To make mother and daughter whole. People take comfort in these reconciliation stories; they can't manage the black and white of it, the possibility that love can be extinguished, that, when continuously tested, love can dissolve. Love is conditional. People need simple answers from me: that I am filled with regret, that I'm lost without her, that I love her still. I want to explain that the last time I felt safe was when I was nine, before cocaine, before it hurt to love her. With her, love and fear were one and the same, with every kiss came a pinprick, with every hug came a lashing out. My mother was my first hurt.

I want to tell Anne that loving my mother was killing me.

But instead I say, "It's better for me that I don't."

"Find her or forgive her?" Anne asks.

"Is there a difference?"

Anne buttons a button. I see the interlocking *C*s: Chanel.

"Anyway, I'm better now. Ironically, I have a certain *closure* with her loss. And I think this is healthy, my having moved on."

"I see," she says.

You see nothing. You will see what I want you to see. I return to my PowerPoint presentation of accomplishments, to prove to Anne all that I've overcome. See me now. I'm complete, nothing missing.

"It's admirable, all that you've done," Anne says.

"And I didn't need my mother for any of it," I say.

"Your therapist—she felt your work was done?" Anne scribbles in her notebook.

"*I* felt I was done," I say.

Anne stops writing and looks up at me. She opens her mouth and the air in the room turns. It smells of trunks in attics, toys locked up in basements, of moths, frantic, flittering in cobweb-laced windows. It smells of places you don't want to go.

THE SKY ISN'T VISIBLE FROM HERE

"You had to be strong for what you went through," Anne says, pensive.

"Like a warrior," I say.

On the subway, I pause in the middle of the closing doors. One foot in the subway car, the other on the platform, and it suddenly bothers me that I can't tell if I should be creating new life when I've been throwing my existing one away.

"IT'S CAVIAR. *Beluga!*" Merritt says. "And don't even get me started on how much it cost." The caviar is set on a serving platter of crushed ice resembling diamonds; lemon wedges serve as garnish. We are in a restaurant below street level, somewhere downtown, I suspect. Merritt scoops up a dollop with a dainty silver spoon.

"Isn't caviar essentially fish eggs? You're expecting me to eat children? *Babies?*"

"This coming from a woman who snorts rat poison or whatever else they mix your shit with." Merritt laughs.

A waiter refills our glasses with chilled vodka. There are now two Merritts, twins. I keep drinking, hoping for triplets.

"Okay, Sally Struthers. Save the Children. One egg at a time."

"What's so wrong with that?"

Merritt sighs extravagantly, as if the answer is obvious to everyone but me. "You can't always be the mother, Felicia."

"YOU LIE ALMOST as well as I do. *Almost,*" she says. In this dream, we are in bed. My mother strokes my hair as if it's the first time she's touched it. "I've never seen it this straight. It used to take me a goddamn hour to fix you in the morning. How did you get it this way?"

"You've got to go," I say, yanking off the comforter. She won't budge.

"Go where? This is home."

I push pills onto my tongue. "This is not your home."

"Lisa, do you have . . . What was it that you said, the fancy word you used, queen of the fancy words? Oh yes, *closure*. Tell me," my mother asks, gesturing at the small space between our sleeping bodies. "Would you call this *closure*?"

I swallow the contents of the bottle whole.

My mother smirks, snatching the empty bottle from my hand. "You're already asleep. What good are those going to do you now?"

"Go away," I say. "I don't want you here."

"By the way, I should tell you, your coke's for shit. It's so stepped on I can see the fucking *footprints*. I had so much better."

"You always have to have had it better," I say, bolting out of bed.

Awake now, I rummage through crates and totes, old suitcases and duffle bags, until I find her photo album, a thin gray book with gummed pages. In the back, poking up through the plastic, is a huge clump of hair, braided and bound neatly by colorful rubber bands. Saved from a time when my locks were shorn and tight curls crept up behind my ears. I flip and flip, but nothing. No family, only a few grainy photographs of my mother stepping out of a car, and dozens of mangled shots—punched-through faces, severed limbs. My mother made it a habit to cut people out of photographs once they hurt her. When you wronged her, when she left you, you ceased to exist. You were excised from snapshots, and all that was left was your hand on her shoulder that she couldn't cut out, a toe curled next to hers. My mother was an artisan with a scissor.

"Why couldn't you leave me with *something*," I say out loud, to the dark, empty room, "with something other than cut-up photographs of *you*?"

THE FOLLOWING WEEK I meet with a doctor. Same building, same elevator, another floor.

"You're completely healthy. Cholesterol is low, your blood counts are within range, platelets are normal, and of course, your HIV test came back negative. Your sodium levels are a smidge high but nothing to get too concerned about."

"Great, so when do I start donating eggs?" More important, when should I expect to receive a check?

The doctor chuckles. "It's a little bit more complicated than that." She outlines the procedure: the daily injections, the hormones to speed up egg production, the fact that it could take three months before one is even fertilized in vitro. She warns about long-term risks: ovarian cancer and infertility. Although cases of infertility are rare, she tells me to consider this should I want children.

Until now I haven't considered children and the possibility of my having them. I'm too selfish for a pet, even fish. I've killed cacti. "Let the egg factory begin," I joke.

The doctor reviews my paperwork and pauses. "Let's talk more about your medical history. Your family's history."

I answer most of her questions with a standard no or not to my knowledge, yet when I'm about to lie about the leukemia on my maternal side (my mother told me her father had died from it, but who really knows?), I pause. It would be so easy to concoct a healthy family, but suddenly I begin to feel uneasy, picturing the faces of two expectant parents and the possibility of a child with a cancerous organ, an amphetamine addiction, or a birth defect. The guilt, the weight of it, is entirely too much to bear. Those strangers don't deserve my children.

For the first time in years, I tell the truth. How I don't know my real father's identity. When I was nine, my father was Peruvian; when I was thirteen, he was American Indian; and when I was eighteen, he was the man who raped my mother. But none of this was true because with my mother, you never knew what to believe; she had a convenient story for every occasion. My aunt Carmen once told me he was Italian, charming—he spoke with his hands, like me. I know nothing about myself. I lack origin. I only know that I look exactly like my mother.

"Maybe I shouldn't risk it," I say. "I don't think it would be fair. For the parents, I mean."

"Don't you have brothers or sisters?"

"I'm an only child."

"Aunts, uncles? Other family members you could interview," the doctor presses.

"My aunt Carmen, but she moved away when I was twelve,

to exactly where I don't know. I don't even know her last name. Our grandmother had so many children from different men — my mother once said our family was a race rainbow. Scary, isn't it, to not know your aunt's last name? But now there is no one else, not anymore. My mother made sure of that." I laugh darkly. "I'm the only one left."

"There must be someone," she says.

"There is *no one*," I say, sounding both contrived and dramatic.

"I'm kind of in a bind here," she says. "Without a definitive history . . ."

"But what if we told them all of this, what we know about me, up front, what then?" I remember the eight thousand. "I'm healthy. What if that was enough to go on?" And then I realize a family isn't a roulette table, a deck of cards. A woman's body isn't a casino.

"I'm afraid that it won't be enough," she says.

"Maybe I should go."

"It's so unfortunate, Felicia. You were otherwise the perfect candidate."

"Isn't it always that way?" I say, and make my way to the door.

My APARTMENT IS above a famous Italian restaurant where every night a serenade of "That's Amore!" or a guitar strumming the Godfather theme greets tourists. There are no menus, just vast courses of cheese-soaked pastas and greasy cutlets served on platters, a carousel of overpriced food that is everything but Italian.

There are rats on the ground floor; I've seen them tear through plastic bags and loaves of bread. Sundays, vomit and crushed tomatoes cover the sidewalk. Below me live club kids turned drug dealers. They still listen to Elastica and Garbage, talking about dime bags that no longer cost ten dollars. Above me is an old widow who plays Chinese arias until early morning. If I leave my window open, I can hear her weeping.

Merritt tells me that she's been fired. Her boss caught her snorting Ritalin in the executive conference room. She's lying on my bedroom floor, tossing my stuffed animals in the air.

Tonight we're sour, edgy, off-kilter.

"What were you doing with *Ritalin*? Poor man's coke," I say. Pointing to my plush monkey dressed in a flannel robe in midair, I snap, "Stop with that."

"Why do you have all these stuffed animals?" she asks. "Collecting them past the age of five is not normal."

"And Ritalin in the conference room is?"

"You'd do it if you had it," she says.

"I'd at least wait until I got home. You have to have rules, Merritt."

"You and your rules."

"*I* still have a job." After having recently been fired from a failed dot-com, it took me three months to find my new job. I'm on a leave of absence from the Columbia writing program; I'm not sure when I'll be ready to return. After a semester, I left midday binge drinking and late-night drug taking and many horribly written short stories behind. I needed to breathe before I could write.

"Only because they don't know you. They know your other face," Merritt says. "It must be exhausting to be you all day long."

"I'm over it. I'm done," I say.

"I've heard that line before. What, your dealer's on vacation? He cut you off?"

"He rolled up with his ten-year-old son. He sold me three grams while his son was in my room with my stuffed animals. It was *ghetto*."

"He does what he has to in order to survive. By any means necessary," Merritt says. "He's one of us, a warrior."

"We're cowards," I say.

"Speak for yourself," Merritt says curtly. She rises, puts on her shoes. I recognize them, the faux crocodiles with the ankle straps; she bought them with me at Barneys. In a lunchtime high, we raced uptown and charged two thousand dollars for six pairs of shoes, returned to work with a ticker tape of receipts clutched in our fevered hands.

"You don't even know who *you* are," Merritt says, winding her scarf around her neck. I imagine Merritt hanging herself in her closet, a cord of expensive cashmere lassoed around her neck.

I tell my drug buddy that, for the first time since we've met, we agree on something.

In my dream, my mother calls my name as if it is the first time she's ever said it. She's weary. We meet at eye level. Her face reveals itself to me; a few lines crease her forehead, a small pimple dots the bridge of her nose. She has large pores. My mother has the kind of lips you want to keep kissing. Barely audible, she tells me she's lost; she doesn't know where she is. She doesn't know how she got here, in me, in my sleep.

"You're asking the wrong person," I say, "I'm just as lost as you are."

My mother sits at the foot of my bed and unbraids her hair. "I'd like to talk to you. I'd like for us to have an actual conversation," she says.

"If I ever doubted I was dreaming . . ."

"How long do you plan on mourning me?" she asks. "I'm getting tired of being dragged around your life. Blamed for everything."

"I don't know," I say. "I've never *not* mourned you."

In a quieter voice, she says, "I guess it's too late for an apology."

"As if an *I'm sorry* will change everything." I ask her about the children, the blond, easy hair, and the ripe skin.

My mother throws her arms up in the air. "You're asking me to explain your dream? That's all you, those kids ain't got nothing to do with me." As soon as I open my mouth, she says, "And don't go correcting my grammar."

"I wouldn't dream of it."

"You have so many nice things," she says, her voice seared with envy. Wandering my room, she opens and closes dresser drawers. She rubs cedar blocks in her palms. The price tags would shock her. She fingers crystal-beaded skirts, sniffs shoes in their boxes. She takes one heel out, slips her foot in.

"I earned those things. All of them."

"I have no doubt," she says, pausing.

There is so much I want to ask. But I first want to know this: Have you ever been happy, and did I ever play a role, even a minor one, in that possible happiness? But all that comes out is this: "Are you happy?"

"It doesn't matter if I'm happy, Lisa," she says. "Maybe you should ask yourself whether *you* are."

"One of us has to change," I plead, watching my mother slip away. "At least call me by my given name. You owe me that."

Before she fades completely, dissolving into the carpet threads or tiptoeing out to the fire escape, whichever way she decides to sneak out this time, she whispers, "Lisa, why does it have to be me?"

Where the Boys Go

BOYS CALLED ME SHORTY. Sometimes they whispered, "*Boriqua sexy,*" but mostly they just puckered their lips and snapped the back of my bra as I walked past, or sprayed me with fluorescent water guns in the twilight. I was a white girl, but not too white, who could pass because of all the kinks in my black hair and because I could navigate their tongue.

The summer before junior high school, my goal was to swim from one end of the sixteen-foot public pool to the other. When I wasn't in my bathing suit, I practically lived in a gray acid-washed skirt set that my best friend Violet gave me. On the front of the shirt were the words Next Exit, and the outfit clung to me in unexpected places—tight at the waist, hugging my hips, and loose on top—but I wore it proudly. Acid wash was huge in 1987, stylish, even, and until I'd acquired such a fashionable piece of clothing, I had dressed in acrylic sweaters with pink teddy bears stenciled on the front or cheap sweatshirts that pilled after one washing.

Violet's mother, Ruth, took her to all the cool shops: Joyce Leslie, Rainbow, and sometimes they even ventured into the city to Macy's. Violet always reported the monthly shopping trips in painfully elaborate detail—which subways they took, descriptions of all the placards and billboards in Manhattan, and God forbid if there was a sale—and she hoarded shopping bags under her bed. The plastic bags were folded in two and stacked in neat piles.

Violet lived around the corner from a bodega that sold chicken thighs for a dollar apiece; the cashier wrapped the meat in brown butcher paper so you felt less poor. Old men sat on milk crates, leaning on their canes, hats shielding their eyes, and talked about how the neighborhood was changing, muttering under their beer-stenched breath about the drugs coming in, the loud music, *coño*, the fast cars.

Violet and I had first met in April at the pizza parlor across from Sunset Park. Boys strutted in, bouncing their boomboxes on their shoulders, the laces yanked out of their new Adidases. They beat-boxed to Slick Rick and Doug E. Fresh's "Lodi Dodi." They took over the tables and feasted on pepperoni pizzas, plantain chips, and Sunny Delight. Violet picked at her knee scabs, skin flaking on her stool. When she caught me staring, she winked and said, "Want to know how I got them?" Although I didn't even know her, something told me I didn't want to hear the story. Violet got up, plopped herself across from me in the booth. Turning my straw upside down, she began to slurp.

I told her I didn't have germs.

"It's not you I'm worried about," she said, finishing my drink.

At that time I lived a few avenues down from Violet, another world, it seemed. Boys had ribbon curls, and even in the summer, girls dressed in wool skirts that grazed their ankles. Hassids minding Shabbat retreated indoors when they heard the Friday alarms blaring at sundown. I imagined this was what war must sound like. I peered out my window to observe this weekly ritual, my neighborhood reduced to candlelit enclosures. There was quiet in the evening except for the crickets mating in the trees and my mother clanging skillets on the hot plate. The air outside smelled of pastry, of things baking. The Jewish girls glared at my shorts, mocking me. They played double Dutch and ignored me when I begged to be included. They were haughty when I offered them chips, turned up their noses at my Lisa Frank sticker collection.

Every summer my mother tried to keep me hidden, tucked inside.

"Why do you need friends?" she kept asking. "You have me. You don't need anyone else." My mother said this when she was envious of my sticker collection and started hoarding more expensive albums of her own, showing off her chocolate scratch-and-sniffs, the lush Lisa Franks, the aqua bubble stickers. Her albums were always so much more beautiful than mine. "I'm the only friend you need." She yelled this when she spied my lanyard key chain, and then she brought home a box of the colorful plastic from which she fashioned dozens of key chains and bracelets while my allowance thinned. In a small voice I kept pleading for her to let me out. And when she finally did, that's when I met Violet. She was the first real friend I had.

"Meet me at ten at the park," Violet said one Saturday in July. "And for *Chrissake* don't wear that green bathing suit. I'm not rolling with Kermit the Frog."

I gripped the phone cord with my fingers. The green terry-cloth suit had been a birthday present from my aunt Marisol a few years ago, before her eyes and fingers turned yellow. The trunks had faded and the top was tattered, but I had nothing else.

After a long pause, Violet sighed into the phone and said, "Come over, you can borrow my mom's one-piece. Ruth's having one of her *episodes*. She's so out of it she won't even notice." Violet's mother was a drug dealer who broke the unspoken cardinal rule: Never dip into your own supply.

At the pool, Violet would shimmy up to lifeguards in her polka-dot bikini. Her long, thin limbs were splotchy with sunburn from the spots she had missed with lotion. She had only one flaw: Violet had chubby toes, fat sausage ones, and she hated their not being symmetrically shaped as toes should be, that, to her horror, the second toe was significantly larger than the big toe. Socks always covered her feet, even at the pool. Before she'd slide her naked feet into the water, she would leave a pair of thick white socks on the pool's edge.

In the water, she'd invite grown men to come closer with her violet eyes while I cowered in the background. I'd look at her, then at myself, my hair all frizzy corkscrews, one arm a little shorter than the other from a car accident last year when I was ten. While my mother was in a Laundromat, I had run across the street and the next thing I remember I was lying on the ground. My collarbone was shattered and wasn't set right in its cast and, while one arm continued to grow, the other became slightly stunted. It was barely noticeable then, but in later years the difference in length would be significant.

Boys at the pool would tell me that I'd be beautiful, really beautiful—if only I had Violet's face, her feathery hair, her silver rings on my fingers. And I closed my eyes and lived the rest of the summer like that, her head in mine, on mine.

Outside Sunset Park, after swimming, I crafted short stories on loose-leaf paper. I described glass pipes, aluminum foil, and tumblers of rum half-filled. I wrote about my first drink, from a bottle of champagne at my baptism party when I was five. I had twirled around, clutching the heavy bottle with two hands, taking swigs, while my mother stood in a corner encased in smoke. Everybody toasted me, their glasses of Bacardi raised high, sweat on their lips. "Cheers," they said. "Finish the bottle," they clamored, until my mother finally turned around and laughed. "That's my girl," she said as I staggered closer, my baptism gown soiled and smelling of spilled wine. I reached for her, but she had already turned away.

WHEN I WAS EIGHT, while I waited for my mother to pick me up after work, my aunt shot up in the bathroom with the door wide open. Marisol fiddled with a syringe, poked at a pus-filled abscess on her upper arm, trying to find a vein, any vein. I could be here or not here—it wouldn't matter. It was only Marisol, alone with her drugs.

You accepted these things as fact: Normal people shot heroin in their arms, in the spaces between their toes, in their neck. This was normal. *This was normal.* You kept repeating that to yourself as you played house with Big Michelle, the blond-haired plastic doll with the blue eye that fell out, the doll that towered over you. When the meth addicts dropped by, raking their arms because of the itch, you colored in the lines of your coloring books with crayons that had exotic names like honeydew and cobalt. "Well, if it's not normal, then it's like pictures in a storybook," you mouthed to Michelle, "it's not real." Saying that helped you sleep but failed to prevent the nightmares: oceans of blood so dark it was black, the works, the heads lolling to one side, the white eyes. And your pillowcases were soaked with tears and sweat because you kept dreaming about the dead. You wished that at the age of eight the words *dope sick* and *junkie* did not exist in your vocabulary. You held Big Michelle closer. At school you carted around your Strawberry Shortcake lunchbox all smiles and you prayed that no one would notice. That no one could smell the death in your hair.

I missed the old Marisol. We used to play freeze tag or detective. We hid in closets, buried under clothes and boots worn down to the soles. I loved her running around, her shouting in her thick Spanish accent, "Call me titi," slang for aunt, she'd said; she was someone I always wanted to watch. But heroin made her lifeless, too tired to play. All she wanted to do was sleep.

"Pretty, pretty girl," Marisol said to herself. "I was a pretty, pretty girl." Although it sounded like "pity, pity girl."

I sat on the floor, counting the black and white linoleum squares. Marisol looked up at me, beckoned me toward her. No. No. No. I didn't want to go.

"Come here, I don't bite," she slurred. She grinned as if she knew a secret and it was delicious, naughty.

I tiptoed to Marisol and I kneeled on the floor next to her while she sat on the toilet. She petted my braids, traced the side of my neck. I turned and sniffed her. The inside of her palm was soft; a little wet, it smelled of sweat, and also of tobacco and licorice. We stayed like this for a few minutes, still.

"I'm tired," she said.

"Then go to sleep," I replied.

"I can't." Glancing around the bathroom, her eyes fixed on the shaggy, orange rug in front of her. "Where's your mother? Where's Rose?"

"At work," I said. The hair on Marisol's legs was dark, thick and long. She had apple knees and veins that bulged, forming spider lines on her calves.

"Your mother looks down on me. Thinks she's better. But let me tell you something—I know a thing or two about my sister. And I know a thing or two about your father. Your *real* father."

My eyes widened. What did she know? Whenever I asked about my father, my mother grew quiet. My father was off-limits, forbidden territory. End of conversation. I knew Eddie wasn't my father, but who was? My aunt would give me clues. She'd make a game of it, offering hints of a man I'd never know. She said he had to duck when he entered a room because he was so tall. He had curly hair cut close. He was a joke teller; he could bring a whole house to its knees, have all his friends howling with laughter over his stories. My aunt told me that he wanted to leave my mother, not me.

"Why can't you just tell me his name?" I once asked.

"Don't you know what your mother would do to me?" she said. "But one day, I promise."

Years later, long after Marisol overdosed, I would sit across from my mother in a restaurant while she told me that although my father did leave, he came back. On my second birthday, he knocked on her door, begging to be let in. Through the keyhole she screamed that he wasn't on the birth certificate, he had no daughter, and could he leave before she called the police?

"I wouldn't let him see you after what he'd done to me."

"But it wasn't about you," I said. "He wanted *me*."

My mother shook her head. "How could you forgive a man who leaves?"

We paid the bill. What else could I do? But my mother had stolen my father from me.

"If you only knew," Marisol said now and collapsed into laughter. Her chest rose and fell. She started to violently shake. She coughed and wheezed. I sat on the bathroom floor, while she tried to hold on to me, while I tried to let her go.

But then my aunt left me, as she was prone to do, and drifted away. Before she closed her eyes, she whispered, "Rose isn't a pretty girl. What she did to your father, all those other men, how she had all those men pussy whipped until your father. She drove that poor boy crazy, made him leave. What I would've given to have a man like that."

When my mother arrived at the apartment to take me home, she found Marisol out cold in the bathtub. My mother carried Marisol to bed. She tucked the sheets in and closed the lights.

At home, Eddie was cutting through tough beef. Eddie drove a lemon cab in the day and in the evening used my mother as his punching bag. His presence set her on edge. She waited for a change in his voice, an inflection, anything that could warn her that he was about to snap, because maybe she would have time to lock herself in the bathroom or run out the door.

"Your sister's a fucking junkie," Eddie said.

I nibbled on sticky rice under the table, feeding myself with my hands while watching Eddie and my mother's feet. I refused meat.

"Maybe today will be the day Felicia eats at the table with the rest of us," Eddie said.

"Leave her alone." My mother sighed, handing me dinner while I hid. She wrapped biscuits for me in a paper towel. She sucked her teeth.

Eddie wasn't my father.

"There's something wrong with her," Eddie said. "Children don't eat under tables like goddamn *dogs*."

The chair scraped the floor when she rose to collect the plates. The sound of them collapsing in the sink drowned out Eddie's voice. At that moment, the clang of dishes was a symphony to me, and I was grateful to my mother for such a simple act as clearing the table.

"I think I'll leave Felicia with Jade. That's what I'll do." My mother turned on the ceiling fan, and it sifted the hot air. The kitchen stank of leftovers.

"From a drug addict to an alcoholic," Eddie muttered as my mother closed the bathroom door behind her. "When will you learn?"

Eddie and I sat there, I under the table, he above, sipping our glasses of Coke. We stared at flies getting caught in the brown tape overhead. My mother left Eddie a few months later.

FOR THE FEW YEARS that we stayed with him in his Boro Park apartment, Eddie was still married to his wife, Elizabeth, who lived in a large house in New Jersey. We visited his wife often. On the interstate my legs dangled out the car window, my dress flew up above my knees. Back then, the suburbs were mysterious, exotic, a genteel country that held a great deal of character. Elizabeth lived in a town where people had built-in pools and sliding glass doors and rang in the dinner hour with a round of cocktails, dusk filtering in through pale, gossamer curtains. She resembled the singer Crystal Gayle; she wore wispy Indian-print shirts and was perpetually tanned. Smooth hair the color of charcoal trailed down to Elizabeth's ankles. Diamonds dripped from her tiny wrists and her ears. The first few times we visited, she appeared regal, patrician. Her children were spoiled, prone to fits of shouting and hair pulling. Plush teddy bears and books piled high filled the two girls' rooms.

When I first met Eddie's wife, I had my mother's wineglass in one hand, a stuffed rabbit in the other. I was shy, frightened. We were in Elizabeth's territory — eating food off her plates — and my mother was sleeping with her husband. She basked in our discomfort, was prickly and cold. And for the life of me, I couldn't understand why we kept going back. Why did we repeatedly return to a house where we were clearly not wanted?

Fingering the material of my mother's pale-blue crepe dress, Elizabeth said, "Must be hard to afford new clothes on a waitress salary, Rosita."

"It's *Rosina*." My mother sat in a chair and crossed and uncrossed her legs.

"Caroline, go fill one of those bags with your old books and toys so Felicia can take them home."

"We don't need your *books*," my mother said.

"Caroline, go."

Elizabeth took in my hair. "I keep telling Eddie that this neighborhood isn't what it used to be. Niggers moving in, building houses. And then the half-breeds. White as paper but you can always tell them by their hair. One has to be careful now. They're sneaky, that kind."

I gave my mother her glass, and she took a small, measured sip. Then, setting it down, she said, "My daughter isn't a *nigger,* if that's what you're implying."

When Eddie entered the room, Elizabeth smiled and said, "I wasn't implying anything."

It was a day in late September when my mother told me she was finally leaving him. She grew tired of having her head smashed into the carpet, blood flowing from her nose and ears, phone cords wound around her neck, cereal boxes and cans of tomato soup hurled at her face, her teeth loose shingles. Countless mornings she'd mask her face in heavy foundation to cover the bruises, the gorgeous rainbow of blue and green and purple. I watched her features melting away in the mirror, a metamorphosis in progress. My mother was beautiful to me because she got out of bed, put on her clothes, prepared my lunch, and went to work. She covered her bruises by any means possible. She functioned, *survived* her day—a body perpetually in motion. Sometimes I leaned into her, begged, "Can I feel, can I feel?" She winced, retreated, yelled at me to go away. My mother obsessed over her foundation, slathered it on; it changed her face, darkened it.

"Don't make it worse," she said. After a brief pause, she continued, "Listen to me and listen good. Never let anyone too close. Love just a little but never too much. You hear me?"

My mother packed us up in small suitcases and stacked them neatly outside the front door. Seated across from Eddie, her hands gripping the arms of the leather chair, she told him she was leaving. She'd met a man named Avram who gave her flowers and took her out to eat. From the Hispanics and crack addicts on Ninth Avenue, we were moving to the Hassidic Jews and Italians three avenues down. While we waited for the family to move out of our new home, we were going to stay with my mother's sister Marisol, who lived up the block from Eddie.

"You like your meat Kosher?" Eddie asked, snidely.

While my mother spoke, Eddie leered, tucking pieces of his stringy hair behind his ear. He sat in the other leather chair with his legs splayed, his huge stomach spilling over his trousers. Eddie was the largest man I'd ever seen; he towered over me with his six-foot frame and his 250-plus pounds. A chain-smoker, he always had two cigarettes tucked behind his ear. Eddie was enamored of expensive black wood: Our ceilings were vaulted and painted a rich black, and he purchased a dark dining-room set with deep crenellations and carvings, had it shipped in carefully packed crates from New Jersey. For every time an ash missed the ashtray and landed on any table, my mother would find her face pressed down so hard on the wood that her cheek took on the intricate pattern.

I slid under couches, crawled into cabinets under the sink, any small space I could fit into. I starved myself in hopes of becoming invisible. The morning of my kindergarten graduation, my mother force-fed me scrambled eggs and ketchup. The tines of her fork scrapped my teeth. She cried for me to eat. "Just eat," she begged, over and over. "Don't make a sound. Don't make him angry. Don't make it worse than it already is."

I still have a Polaroid from that day—me in a light blue dress, hands on my hips, pretty-posing for the camera.

I STOOD OUTSIDE in the hallway with our suitcases and bags, peering in. Eddie nodded, pulled a cigarette from behind his ear. When my mother rose, he held out a hand, paused, and said, "You can leave for now—I'll allow that." And then he paused again.

"But I'll find you and then I'll kill you. Then I'll fuck your daughter."

Honey, a homeless forty-year-old crack addict who lived under the basement stairs, walked up and down the hallway, her fingers tracing the cool cement walls. In a cracked, shaky voice, she sang, "Mary had a little lamb, little lamb, little lamb." A week later, the police would find her lying face up with eight-ball eyes, rigor mortis settling in.

I'm leaving.

MY MOTHER WAS TRIUMPHANT. She had suffered with this man for three years and she took pleasure in her departure. For her it meant power. It was a joy and she savored it. For the first time in what seemed like years, I caught her smiling.

At Marisol's I slept with my mother's hand shielding my eyes so I wouldn't wake up and see the fat roaches skittering in front of my nose or my aunt combing the floor for dime bags, pouches with skull and crossbones stamped on the front. We took over my aunt's room and she slept on the couch. Outside, drop-top Impalas cruised up and down the street, bass thumping. On stoops, mothers braided their daughters' hair, sneaking sips of Bacardi from Dixie cups. Their voices traveled up the fire escape. They talked about who was getting out of jail, who was going in, who was going back to school, which of them were getting their GED, because everyone was trying to make a better deal. On TV, we all heard about the rich people—stock markets and Wall Street—we saw them buy houses on Long Island with three-car garages, and we wondered, What about us? Where were our cable boxes and sprinklered lawns?

One night when Marisol's hand slid into my mother's smock, rummaging for dollar bills, my mother moved her hand from my eyes to my ear, and in a husky voice she threatened to cut her sister in two. Marisol laughed her high-pitched laugh but immediately fell silent when my mother rose from the bed and said, "Test me."

Marisol never entered her own room uninvited again.

Years later I would hear a story about how my mother once saw her sister on the other side of the street. Calmly, my mother crossed, walked up to her sister, and lunged for her throat with one hand. My mother kept choking her. It took three men to pry her hands from her sister's neck.

"Sssh," my mother said, crawling back under the covers, drawing me close. "I'll make this all go away." And I fell asleep to the sound of her breath in my ear.

A few days later, Marisol came home with a sack of groceries slung over her shoulder. I watched my aunt's yellowed hands as she unloaded the boxes of pasta, bottles of green olive oil, and hot sausages wrapped in waxed paper. Marisol's fingers made my mother's hands shake, but I was in awe of a woman who could change color. My mother was sober then; she took care of us. My aunt was slight, barely anything but a sheet of skin draped over skeleton. I never saw Marisol eat and she never appeared hungry. But she loved cooking for us, outfitting for a mother role. She'd fix dinners from recipes she saw on TV.

Marisol tried to set the table, but the forks fell out of her hands and onto the floor with a loud *clang*. My mother picked them up, placed them on the table. We could hear Marisol's teeth grinding. She was frantic, pulling strands of hair out of her head.

"Napkins, I don't think I bought the napkins. I mean I saw them, they were in the supermarket, and I knew we didn't have any, that we ran out, but then I had my list from the cooking show and if I just got everything on the list, it would be okay," Marisol said, her voice cracking. "We would be okay, but then I forgot the fucking napkins. So now it's all wrong. Is it wrong, Rose?"

My mother's face went slack. "We can use the paper towels you bought, Marisol," she said softly, and pointed to the six rolls of Bounty poking out from the brown C-Town bags.

For a moment Marisol looked puzzled and stared at the paper towels as if they were alien. "I don't remember *those*." She paused, then pressed on, whizzing about the kitchen, preparing our meal. Her mouth wouldn't stop moving.

"Sit down," my mother ordered. Marisol kept pacing.

"Did I tell you what happened at the Chinese restaurant today?" Marisol asked. She pulled sausage meat out of the casings.

"How could you, you just got home," my mother replied, her shoulders tensed. She bent down, holding her head in her hands.

Marisol hosted at the Midnight Dragon on Thirteenth Avenue. Weekly, without fail, she was fired for going in late or not showing up at all, but Mr. Fong couldn't say no to Marisol. Humbled, she'd crawl back smelling of soap, armed with an exaggerated story, another excuse, another death, another four-car pile-up on New Utrecht—"It was all over the news didn't you see?" And she'd beg poor Mr. Fong for forgiveness, saying *please* over and over until he waved her up to the front. Get back to work.

"Well, *anyway,* old Fong bought one of those mail-order brides for his son, you know, that's how the Chinese do it, marriage, it's all arranged. So they spent all this money on airfare to get her here from China, or wherever these catalogue girls come from, which reminds me that I've never really been on a plane before, but anyway, the bride gets here, and after the first night in bed, the son wakes up and discovers that she has this sickness where her hair falls out. The son woke up and found clumps everywhere. On the sheets, on the pillowcases—*Jesus fucking Christ* can you imagine—it was like a damn fish leaving scales all over the place, Mr. Fong said. So I asked old Fong why couldn't they just send her back to the catalogue where they got her? But then he looked at me funny so I shut up."

My mother and I were speechless.

"Me, I don't buy anything from a magazine," Marisol continued. "I take my ass into the store where I can *see* what I'm getting," my aunt affirmed, shaking pasta boxes like maracas.

Her sudden bursts of energy excited me. Marisol zipped around the apartment, rearranging boxes in cabinets, filling huge pots with water, boiling things. And then there were the quick bathroom breaks. A few moments now and then between dicing the

THE SKY ISN'T VISIBLE FROM HERE

garlic and buttering the bread. And my mother's eyes followed her through the apartment, witness to her sister's bouncing from one drug to another: cocaine, bennies, poppers; and Valium to lighten the inevitable fall. Heroin was special and used only on occasion, at least at first.

Marisol moved so fast that I was out of breath, but suddenly she collapsed, fell into her lime green kitchen chair, and my mother quietly took over: drained the pasta, served it in small bowls, cut us pats of butter. My aunt looked so utterly hopeless and tired; she looked as if she were a house losing all its power—watt by watt, flickering, out. And then my mother propped her feet up on the table and lit a cigarette. She watched her sister sleep.

My mother always cleaned up after her sister, corrected everything.

Two weeks later, she found me with Aunt Marisol's works. At the kitchen table I poked my fingers with the dainty syringe and stirred lentils with the needle. I wore the green bathing suit Marisol had bought for me. Bad Company's "Shooting Star" blared throughout the tiny apartment. My mother yanked me away, threw our clothes into our beat-up suitcases, and we fled down the three flights into the night.

NOON. VIOLET WAS two hours late, as usual. On the way to the park I had stopped at her house. After I rang her bell for over ten minutes, a girl yelled out the window, "Hello! What about *not home* did you not understand?"

The smell of hot dogs and fat sausages was heady, pungent,

and I balanced my lunch between my knees. I preferred my hot
dog with ketchup on a soft bun, and all the boys wanted relish,
kraut, mustard, more of this and more of that—just more. Fill-
ings spilled over the sides of the bread. Lines snaked around the
hot dog cart. Short Dominican women prepared ices flavored with
raspberry or blueberry syrup while their children scurried about,
taunting one another with their pink tongues and ice-blue lips.
All I wanted to do was swim from one end of the pool to the
other, to feel the weight of my body as I dived in headfirst, the
cool water lapping under my ears. To snort chlorine up my nose,
access that brain freeze, the rush that made your eyes squint tight.
Every day, I would leave the pool red-eyed, hungry, and strong.
Already I could slice through the water fast, butterfly stroke it to
midway. I charted my progress. Sometimes there was a moment
when my ears clogged and all the noise, the splashing, the babies'
shrieks, and the parents' shouting—"Don't make me come get
you"—dulled to a soft murmur and I could swim uninterrupted.
I could cleave the water in silence. But Violet always nagged me,
called after me from the diving board, clapping her hands like
a damn seal, urging me to the four-foot kiddie pool, where the
boys lounged, darting around the girls like fleas. The boys walked
like ball players, swaggered from side to side. All the girls sneered
at Violet, talked trash behind her back. "Crazy bitch," someone
would mutter. "*Loca*."

Now she blew in my ear. "Hey, Shorty," she whispered.

"You're late," I said, not looking up from my lunch. "And don't
call me that."

"Ruth was flipping. Turned the damn apartment upside down looking for her gold hoops. Finally she found them in the icebox. What could I do?"

"I rang your bell for *ten minutes*."

"You actually timed it?" Violet smirked. She wore her hair high, in a silver clip. From her bag she revealed a gold lamé one-piece. It dangled from her hand. "For you," she said.

"I'm actually leaving," I said, gathering my paper bag and a half-empty Coke can.

"Come on, I'm sorry, *I'm sorry*," she pleaded, and then pulled out the big guns. "I'll be your best friend."

I acquiesced, rubbed her shiny bathing suit between my fingers.

"Let's go change," Violet said, linking my arm with hers, leading me inside to the pool.

THREE WEEKS AFTER I met Violet, she visited my house. All the shades were pulled. Barely a fraction of light seeped in. My mother was draped on the couch, sipping iced tea and watching her soap operas. As soon as I said Violet's name, my mother said, "So, you're the girl who's responsible for all those lunches she buys. My daughter believes that money grows on trees. Isn't that right, *Felicia*?" She craned her neck toward me and glared.

While she spoke, I looked down at the red carpet. Although we no longer lived with Eddie, our new home on Twelfth Avenue was decorated like his, with the red wall-to-wall carpet and black wood furniture my mother had inherited from him after his death. A conch, a pack of Kent 100s, a porcelain pink mouse, and photographs of Avi, my mother, and me were arranged neatly on the table. A photo album filled with butchered pictures lay on the carpet. There are pictures of me with my arm sliced out, her in that blue crepe dress, Eddie's hair caught in the frame. Years later, she would slash out Avi, too. Her severed history. *My* severed history.

A plastic bookcase next to the stereo housed stacks of vinyl LPs: Eddie Rabbit, Bread, Chi-Lites, and the Commodores. Behind the speakers my mother stashed a collection of porno magazines and a few John Holmes movies that I sneaked and watched when she was at work.

Violet and I shuffled our feet. Violet beamed, flashed rows of pretty teeth, but her charms were lost on my mother, who upped the volume on *General Hospital* and ended the conversation with, "I wonder about the kind of mother who allows her daughter to dress like that." She gestured at Violet's electric-blue tube skirt hiked high. Beauty marks covered her thighs. Already far more developed than her twelve years would suggest, my best friend was a slutty confection of beauty marks smattering her peach skin.

Violet's mouth widened to a large O.

"We're going in my room," I said.

My mother merely increased the volume again.

On my bed, Violet twisted the arms of my teddy bear. "You still play with stuffed animals?"

"I'm sorry about my mother."

"I've heard worse," she said, covering her legs with my sheet.

"She keeps talking about shutting off the phone."

"Maybe your mom and Ruth should go bowling." She laughed

but then paused, becoming quiet, allowing the words to settle between us. In a small voice, she continued, "I got that line from a movie. I wouldn't even know where to find a bowling alley. I've never seen a bowling ball."

And at that moment I wanted to say something, find words to make it all easier, to tell Violet that it was okay that her mother's home was a revolving door of men who called for business. Ruth's bedroom was outfitted with baggies and twist ties, scales and chemicals stored in sterilized glass jars. Pounds of weed, heroin, crack, and pale blue pills were labeled and segregated in dresser drawers. Crack was her best seller, Violet confided, because it hit the junkies quick; your whole body went numb—for only five dollars. Once, I saw a junkie ripping out her toenails, and she didn't cringe once from the pain. And for five dollars a hit, everyone was 'basing. On the first and fifteenth of the month, people clipped past us on their way into Ruth's "office," using their hands to part the beaded curtain. Violet's eyes never left the television; she fixed on the canned applause, the crescendo of laughter. But when the beads crashed together, cordoning in her mother and yet another junkie who'd just cashed his check and was looking for a taste, I could feel Violet flinch.

We were fatherless daughters with mothers who offered little consolation. Maybe that's why we clung to each other so readily. We were girls who hung out in the parks late at night, in overheated pizzeria kitchens, in the back of bodegas, sitting on milk crates and sipping cold beer out of brown paper bags, playing rummy on makeshift tables made of stacked cardboard boxes. We would do anything not to go home, back to those dark cages. We would do anything to escape feeling lonely and scared, because to be with those feelings, to really let them settle, was unimaginable.

One afternoon Violet and I split ices by the pool. We stuck our tongues out at each other, showing off our purple mouths and teeth. We wondered where we'd go, how we'd spend the rest of the day. I offered my house, but Violet shook her head and said, "I'm not welcome there."

"Forget about her," I said.

Violet wrinkled her nose and said, "I know her."

"What are you talking about, 'I know her'? You only saw her a few times."

Violet shook her head. "You don't understand. I've *met* your mother before."

"How do I look?"

"Actually, you look a little skinny," Violet said, surveying my stomach with satisfaction. We sat on wooden benches in the locker room of Sunset Park in our bathing suits. Pointing to my legs, she said, "And you need to start shaving." In response, I rubbed my hairy legs against her smooth ones, and she squealed.

I'd been skipping meals, feasting only on Cheese Doodles for breakfast and fried hot dogs for dinner. When she'd gotten caught stealing out of her diner's cash register, my mother had been fired and had resorted to weekend morning shifts at a luncheonette on Tenth Avenue. She felt this was beneath her—the lousy shifts, the quarter tips—but she bit her lip, tied on her black smock, and headed out at dawn to open. Food began to disappear from our fridge — no more slices of Velveeta, loaves of white bread, or sticky jars of grape jelly. Our refrigerator was anorexic except for a bag filled with potatoes, a stick of butter, a little carton of milk. On the hot plate my mother made home fries, French fries, or boiled potatoes for our meals. She became inventive with a vegetable peeler and those starchy potatoes. Twice my mother applied for welfare and food stamps, but she was rejected. We were months behind in rent.

I'd taken to checking pay phones for dimes, sneaking money out of Ruth's drawers for snacks. I ate chips slowly, took meticulous little bites from soft buns.

"I'm never hungry," I said, and roved the insides of my thighs. My body was leaner, tighter. Nylon lined the gold lamé suit, which hung on me like a dress. Violet stared at me, envious.

"Me neither," she said, adjusting her bikini straps. She turned, scrutinizing herself in the bathroom mirror. "But it's never enough."

When I asked her what she meant, she waved me away, slipped on her sunglasses, and said, "Let's go for a dip."

The concrete was hot against our bare feet. There were two pools on opposite ends of the park, the four footer and the sixteen footer with a diving board. We settled on the four-foot side of the park, where all the boys were. Unattended inflatable donuts and children sporting goggles cluttered the water. I recognized Elsa and some girls from her crew sitting on beach towels, squeezing water out of their thick hair. They had tortured me in grade school, and Violet knew them from the pool. The girls were tawny, voluptuous; they walked with a swish. Violet followed my gaze and snorted, "I heard she's going to Montauk. Too stupid to get into a magnet." In sixth grade, kids took exams in order to apply for magnet schools, junior high schools that specialized in performing arts or the sciences. No one wanted to go to the zoned junior high schools in our area (Pershing or Montauk, depending on which side of New Utrecht you lived on), which were a repeat of elementary—classes held in gymnasiums and bathrooms, thirty-year-old textbooks, substitute teachers. I got accepted to Peter Rouget I.S. 88, a communication arts school in Park Slope. Violet won admission to I.S. 293 in Cobble Hill to study dance.

"She'll be pregnant before high school, and Ruth will probably sell drugs to the rest of them," Violet said, applying baby oil.

Violet eyed a group of boys gyrating and beat boxing to KRS 1. Some shouted out "your momma" jokes. Others cannonballed into the water, splashed all the children and mothers on the sidelines. They ranked on everyone who passed by.

"Remember, Felicia," Violet instructed, smoothing her hair, "only give them tongue. Nothing else."

Give them tongue?

In the water, I grew uneasy. I felt claustrophobic surrounded by so many bodies. The boys traveled in packs, and they soon caught sight of Violet. They were musty and lean, with patches of dark underarm hair. They wore their hair slicked back. One started speaking to me in Spanish. His name was Miguel. He had green eyes. He went to high school.

"I don't speak Spanish," I said, by way of introduction.

"But you *look* Puerto Rican," he said.

"She's Irish," Violet said.

"Shamrocks and shit," said another boy.

"Something like that," I said.

When they asked us where we went, Violet lied and said we went to Midwood. "We're freshmen."

Soon the crowd thinned to Calvin and Miguel.

"Your body is slammin'," Miguel whispered in my ear. "You got mad shape." His breath smelled of meatball heroes, and those lips — they were plump and abnormally pink. God, I hated pink — just last year I'd tacked posters on every inch of my pink walls and filled in the spaces I missed with Magic Marker. When we moved into the apartment, I complained about the pink walls, but my room was the only one Avi wouldn't repaint. I didn't know why.

I listened as Miguel laid his rap on thick. We hadn't spoken for ten minutes and here he was, mapping our future or at least our plans for the next week. Meanwhile he never asked my name. Wednesday we would sneak into the Loew's on Eighty-sixth Street, since that was the only movie theater in Brooklyn we knew of that had a functioning air conditioner. And more important, the ticket agent turned a blind eye to all the kids looking for free entertainment. Thursday we would have cones at Carvel, and Friday, well, Friday, was freestyle. "We could kick it, *parley*." He was talking so fast, I wanted to grab his jaw and say, "Slow down, you just met me. You don't even know my name."

Miguel's lips moved so fast, I felt dizzy. He asked me what my *deal* was. He wanted *information* but never stopped talking long enough to hear the answers. Did I have a boyfriend ("I ain't no appetizer")? Was my mom cool? Did I have friends who were down? Were they fly? And, oh, by the way, did I have a loosie? As if I packed cigarettes in my bathing suit.

I didn't want to be here, with my skin pruning, listening to some boy who couldn't even look me straight in the eyes when he spoke—he talked above my head or beside my ear. I longed for the sixteen-foot pool on the other side of the park. Ignoring Miguel, I watched bodies fly off the diving board.

Meanwhile, Violet had wandered off to the other end of the pool and was being mauled by Calvin. They looked vulgar, cartoonish, something out of a soap opera, with their passionate embraces, hair raking, and skin against skin. Nauseous and fascinated both, I hardly noticed when Miguel came closer.

"*Dame lengua,* Shorty," he said.

"What?" I said, pulling away.

"*Lengua. Lengua.* Tongue," Miguel said. "Damn, why do you got to go ruinin' my game?"

"Asking for my *tongue* is supposed to be smooth? That's your game?" Who was this Miguel, asking for something so personal so publicly? I didn't belong here, in the shallow end, following my best friend's rules of the pool.

"What's up with you? Why you buggin' out?"

This was a mistake. I swam to the underwater stairs and climbed out.

Miguel shouted, "Why can't you be more like your friend? Why can't you be more like *her*?"

AND THEN VIOLET stopped returning my phone calls. She avoided me completely. She and Calvin had become an item, but rumor had it that she was just tagging around. Calvin owned a car, a 1973 Oldsmobile, and he drove her down Fourth Avenue with the windows rolled down, the sound system up. Exposé and Lisa Lisa and The Cult Jam blasted from the speakers. Tia, a permanent fixture on the stoop, confessed that Violet followed Calvin everywhere.

"Her head be out the window waiting for the horn beep," Tia said, picking her teeth. A clutter of tiny White Castle boxes surrounded her bare feet. "My brother knows him. Calvin goes to Montauk, or goes once a *month,* you know how it be. Nothing but a player. A dumbass with no education. That girl—your *friend*—is getting herself played." Tia burst out laughing. "Played like a record."

Tia also told me about the fighting, the midnight beatings. Ruth and Violet stayed up all hours of the night, throwing chairs, kicking walls. No one in the building knew why they fought; they just heard the screaming and the thumping through the floorboards.

Still, people kept getting buzzed up all night long. Business was booming.

I wrote Violet letters and slid them under her door. She'd ended our friendship so abruptly, and I needed to know why. I didn't believe that it was about Miguel, the pool, the tongue. "Just be honest," I wrote at the end of all my letters. "Just tell me." But my letters went unanswered and Ruth never let me in.

"You're up early," my mother said, fixing her face. She leaned into the sink and coated her lashes with blue mascara.

"I'm going swimming," I said, packing a book bag with books, papers, and white towels.

"At eight in the morning?" She capped the mascara and glanced out the window. The apartment was quiet save for her chewing her gum and dousing Chanel No. 5 on her neck, wrists, elbows, legs. My mother showered herself in a thick mist—she knew no limit when it came to perfume.

"Take an umbrella, then," she said, kicking the door shut.

The sky was silvery, sorrowful shades of gray and blue and the possibility of improvement. Everywhere I looked, I saw signs of demolition and creation. Manhattan developers had been coming in with blueprints, making plans to rejuvenate Boro Park, which was filled with ramshackle houses, crumbling apartment buildings, bodegas, and synagogues. They would build old-age homes and office buildings, clean up parks. So much potential, the developers must have thought, but midway they'd come to see my neighborhood for what it was: small and used, like a woman's lipstick kissed off, a place worth abandoning. Dust and rubble lay everywhere, and the bricks only came up to my knees. As I walked uphill to Seventh Avenue, the sky darkened to a deep bruise, and it began to pour. My tiny umbrella couldn't bear the weight of it, so I tossed it in the gutter. I continued on to the park. Shielded by a bodega's awning, an old man sat on a plastic crate clutching a bottle of Colt 45, his legs spread, his other hand resting on his knee. Unfazed by the storm, he took a long swig and tipped his Marlboro Man hat to me as I sped past.

The rain lightened to a drizzle. The pool was open.

The squish-squish of my blue jelly shoes echoed through the changing room, and I was surprised that my bathing suit, which was safely tucked in my bag, was dry and slightly warm. I stood nude in front of the long mirror and turned from side to side. I ignored the hunger pangs. The reflection showed skin that wouldn't tan, an ivory face, a corpse-white body with ribs jutting out, stomach caving in. And if I squinted just right, I looked the image of my aunt Marisol.

Outside, a custodian collected bubble-gum wrappers and crumbled napkins and shoved them into her trash bags, whistling as she worked. I made my way to the sixteen-foot pool. There were no lifeguards in sight. I dipped my toe into the water, feeling the temperature.

"Never inch yourself into the water," Marisol always warned. "Like ripping off a Band-Aid, jump in quick. It's torture otherwise."

I plunged in, skimmed the bottom of the pool, and swam up to the surface. Breaststroking, I made my way across. It felt easier this time than last; my muscles had grown used to the repetitive motions, the work.

Suddenly Violet was here, shouting. I swam to the pool's edge, peered up. There she stood on the other side of the black gate, arguing with Calvin. She didn't look pretty, her hair falling in frizzy waves. Her legs resembled straws sticking out below her purple miniskirt. She looked *used*. Her beauty marks were a violent rash that spread across her legs. Calvin kept telling her to chill, to calm the fuck down. I couldn't make out the entire conversation, but one thing I heard loud and clear: "You don't want me anymore, do you?" Her voice shrill, she kept repeating the question until Calvin backed away and then fled. Before he took off, he told Violet that she was crazy.

I watched my friend collapse, her face exploding with tears.

IN SEPTEMBER THE POOL in Sunset Park closed for the season, padlocks sealing all the gates. Men arrived and drained the water. The inside of the deeper pool was painted a pale blue, flecked with rust, which I never noticed when the pool was filled. I never did butterfly across. School was starting, and I had bought a new backpack, loaded it with clean spiral notebooks, pens, fresh erasers, and a black loose-leaf binder.

September also ushered in hope. My mother started a new job as a deli manager in Manhattan. "Park Avenue," she cheered. "Four hundred dollars a week!"

Avi approved: "Money, good money." He once told me that certain sidewalks in the city shimmered because the cement was mixed with diamonds. In Manhattan, people were rich; they wore cashmere and silk, held teacups with two fingers, wiped their pretty mouths on linen napkins. They ate food I couldn't pronounce or had never seen.

"We're moving up," my mother assured me.

A week before school started, I went to Violet's house. I slipped through the front door as someone was coming out and made my way up the stairs to the third floor, and I knocked, even though the door was wide open. Violet was lying on the floor, her legs bloodied and twitching. With a knife, she had carved *X*s up and down her calves and on the insides of her thighs.

"Violet?" I said, cotton-mouthed.

For a moment she looked at me as if I were a stranger, but then she smiled and carved another *X*. "Here I am," she said, and pointed to her legs. "See, I'm here."

All I could say was *Oh, my God, Oh, my God.* My hands shook as I leaned in, and I might have asked what she was doing or why she was doing this, or I might have begged her to come with me—I honestly don't remember.

Violet pointed the tip of her blade at me and warned me not to come any closer. She kept saying, "It's too hard."

"Where's Ruth?" I asked. I could barely feel my legs; they were just limbs excised from my body, moving on their own.

Violet clapped her hands as if I'd asked the funniest thing she'd ever heard. She was so loud.

"Ruth's out. She's been *out* for thirty-six hours. 'Based out of her fucking mind." Violet stabbed the air in the direction of the amber beads. "Go in there, see for yourself." A small pool of blood eddied around her. Her violet eyes seemed to blacken.

It was sultry in the apartment, so humid that the walls seemed to sweat.

I parted the curtain. Ruth was sprawled across the bed, feet dangling off the mattress. "See what happens," Violet shouted from the kitchen, "when you fuck with your own supply!" I stood in the living room between Violet and her mother and didn't know where to go. I pulled the phone from its cradle. Violet kept screaming while I called 911.

When the ambulance came, Ruth was still unconscious. They carted Violet away on a gurney. The neighbors gathered on the stoop outside, trading stories, making them up. Kids wheeled their bikes around the police car that arrived. It was a goddamn carnival outside, a fucking parade. I could hear them all from the window. And for the brief moment that I was alone in Violet's apartment, I took off my shoes and socks and stepped in her pool.

Cut

THERE MUST ALWAYS BE ORDER. And when you force yourself awake at nine after colliding with the pillow only two hours before, you bolt up, and a hailstorm of shirts and designer shoes ensues. There is no time for food. You have precisely twenty-five minutes to make it downtown for the meeting you scheduled. You call a town car that races down Park, and finally you dash into the building and flash your identification and collapse inside the elevator. At your desk you have the shakes, and explain to your boss who worries that you may be coming down with something — "You don't look well," he says — that you no longer feel sick and that you're just fine and here is your completed project plan to prove it. He has just returned from a trip to Jerusalem, where he witnessed a car bombing, bodies soaring through the air in front of an out-door café.

Here on your desk is the stack of business cards that read Felicia C. Sullivan, Project Manager. This is 2001 and you work at a ven-ture capital-backed dot-com. The cards' presence somehow com-forts you. Why can't you stop shaking? You know logically that your body is here, but you can't feel it—your lips are numb, limbs slack, toes smothered in these crocodile shoes. And when you talk about milestones, forecasts, and budgets, you get your first nose-bleed. Your boss winces and hands you his clean napkin and says *wipe here, wipe there.* In the bathroom, curled up in the tightest ball you can imagine, you wonder how it is that you got to this point. Because you told yourself in your bathroom that first time in December when you threw the housewarming party, and people came who weren't invited, people trickling in off the street, and you were alone with Merritt in the bathroom with the cracks on the ceiling, the chips hailing down, with two rolled bills and neatly cut lines, that you'd never be an addict like your mother because you survived the war that was her, because you convinced yourself you were stronger than she was. And then, there go the lines.

MONTHS BEFORE I would take a leave of absence from Columbia and months before I would try to sell my eggs to buy cocaine, Emily and I are sitting at the bar in Café Taci, on 110th Street, smoking cigarettes and eating our chicken cutlet parmesans. Emily toys with her food, preferring languorous cigarette ex-halations instead. We met in the writing division office in Dodge

Hall, both embittered by the bureaucratic process that was Columbia registration, first-year graduate fiction students and already we felt tortured, disenfranchised by not winning our workshop selections.

Emily shivers in her pink leather jacket, auburn hair cropped to her ears. She always powders her face to appear pallid, her plum lips and kohl eyes rendering the image of a china doll, an insecure one who feeds on codependent relationships and hoards minor affections like trading cards.

I glance at my watch. Lately my days have become difficult to negotiate—four years out of college and I'm a graduate student in the morning, an executive in the afternoon, and the star at cocktail hour. It's starting to feeling as if I'm in a dressing room and none of the clothes fit. I get the tremors often, and chest pains have become as natural as breathing.

We reminisce over my housewarming party two months back: who attended (all the first years, including the reclusive poets), who drank too much (everyone), who hooked up with whom (who can remember? but there are rumors), and we determine that it was a success. Now we plan a screw-the-snow party to usher in the new term.

I tell Emily about my friend Merritt. I relay the bathroom incident in detail: Merritt and I huddled over the toilet seat, cutting up the contents of a plastic pouch, rolling up ten-dollar bills, crouching, snorting, and dabbing under our noses with tap water. How it all felt very *Less Than Zero* without all the dying. And when I half-jokingly mentioned this to Merritt, she reminded me that cocaine alone didn't kill anyone in the book, *it was freebase that did Julian in.* Confused, I said, "but he doesn't die in the book, only in the movie." "Well, then," she said, "we're safe as houses."

"So what was it like?" Emily asks, plotting out on a cocktail napkin the names of people we would invite.

We hear the jackhammers and power drills outside, shaking bodies handling great machines, cracking the pavement, spilling hot tar. "It's like Broadway up my nose," I say.

What I fail to tell Emily is how many times I've tried it since. And although I savored my first glass of red wine and the many that followed, cocaine is different. I like—no, I *love* cocaine. I tolerate the nausea, the constant swallowing, the teeth grinding—anything for that rush when the world seems simple, beautiful, and large enough to fit me in it. That first night two months ago repeats itself clearly to me each time I use. Right down to how I bit my lip so hard it bled because I never felt so *happy*. After the first bump of coke, I stared at the mold spores flowering across the ceiling, the white paint chipping, raining down in pellets, and the hairline cracks sprouting on the tiles—witness to the crumbling of my cheap apartment, and I thought I could fix it all, clean it up and build anew. With a few coats of paint, plaster, and a spatula, all could be resolved. I would break through the wall to build a window if I had to. Let in some light. I would fix everything.

Already far gone is the awkward, stammering girl who never feels smart enough, white enough, pretty enough. Gone are the images of my mother and her sister Marisol; my high school tormentors with their cruel taunts: *Stinky, Fro, Thief.* A new woman has emerged, breathless, effusive, confident, talking madly with her hands.

"Is it like pot?" Emily is intrigued.

"Coke's not like anything."

Nodding, she combs her hair with her fingers. "I'm curious. Why did you try it? I mean, your mom and everything."

I see my mother's shoulders quake, remember her nose, the bleeding, everything always stained red. Nights I see her hands slithering into my drawers, snatching my paper-route money. Her rent money squandered on glassine bags. I wince.

Dead calm, I reply: "I'm nothing like my mother."

IN A CAB headed downtown, Carlo, the overseas sales rep at the company, asks my coke buddy Merritt and me if we've ever smoked coke. We take swigs from a cheap bottle of Merlot. No, we say. And for a moment I wonder whether normal people chug whole bottles of wine in taxis. Apparently, nobody cares.

"You can't even imagine," he says.

Inside his apartment, we listen to Kruder and Dorfmeister, alternating tracks with the trash they play in the European discos. We wrinkle our noses. We hate this shit, we say. All electronic and thrashing beats, music for meth heads. The plan is to score a few lines and head out to Spa, a club where one bathroom fits three, but Carlo is lying on his couch with a pipe, saying, "You don't know what life is."

Our legs bounce. Our knees knock. Merritt taps her watch and mouths, "Let's *go!*"

Carlo's apartment is starkly furnished: a glass table, steel chairs, lacquer and marble. The two thousand square feet reeks of modernity with its cold austerity, a home much too grand for one person. Our company pays for this apartment in Gramercy Park, a home base for those jetting in from the European offices, a place to crash, host parties, and smoke. Unbeknownst to our employers, they're paying for our addictions. Town cars, phoned in from the office after seven so we can expense them, ferry us to our dealers, to extravagant lunches with designers and advertising agencies that always include a few bottles of good wine. And the money, so much of it, what do you do with all this money at twenty-five?

Lately Carlo has been showing up for meetings jittery, clumsy, all sweaty hands, buttons undone. Sometimes he doesn't show up at all. Yesterday during a meeting, when all his papers scattered over the floor and his hands shook so much that he couldn't manage the conference phone, I leaned over and whispered to a co-worker, "Kill me if I ever get like that."

She scribbled on a piece of paper, slid the note under my folder, "We'll never get like that."

"Try this," Carlo says now, working a pipe. "Believe me, you'll never have better."

"Why do men always say that?" I say. Tonight I feel glamorous, omnipotent. Instead of smoking, I lap lines up like candy. How sweet the numb is on my tongue.

Merritt ransacks empty cabinets. "Do you have anything to drink?"

AT THE BEGINNING of my second semester at Columbia, I'm sitting in a class taught by a celebrated journalist who keeps repeating that every writer is a liar. Reporters offer half-truths, tampered facts, and their own subjectivity. Our job, my professor says, is to distinguish liars by degrees. I have no idea what any of this means, so I reprogram my Palm Pilot.

As my professor rattles off obscure quotes from Plato and Descartes, everyone else hangs on his every word, practically salivating; I'm bored, unimpressed. I'm convinced that I've flushed thirty-five thousand dollars down the toilet.

Later, in workshop, a girl writes on the last page of my short story: "Invest in a grammar book, preferably for beginners, and a dictionary." Instead of a story critique, she staples on a photocopied page from Strunk and White on proper comma usage.

After class we drink well into the evening, until our speech slurs. Kids from Harvard and UCLA shoot pool in the bar and talk coherently about authors they've never read, philosophies they don't know.

At home I pick up *The Waves* and soon I see double, and then I pass out.

I'M LYING ON a park bench; the cool air pricks my skin, dries my dampened shirt. I practice opening my mouth and closing it. I've lost my way. The insides of my nostrils are dry, laden with cracked, scabbed skin and dried blood. Has it always been this way? Perhaps it's been dry all along and I just haven't noticed.

The way you don't notice fruit discoloring, shriveling, caving in on itself until it is covered in mold. Next to me dead leaves crowd a little pond. Scum gathers on the surface.

Today I was fired. Gone are the business cards with my name embossed, the airy office and catered lunches. I hold the stack of cards on my stomach and wonder who I am if I don't have a business card. As an adult I've rarely known what it's like to *not* work. Not to rely on a life of structure, a compartmentalized day filled with project plans and to-dos, breaks for sandwiches and raspberry iced teas.

Over the past month, the owners gradually dismissed each department. The spacious offices pregnant with chatter and mouse-clicking have been reduced to the hum of air conditioners, a lone telephone ringing. Today my final check appeared, Scotch-taped to my door. At midday I left, rode the elevator down and walked thirty blocks to Central Park. I've been here for six hours, mostly sitting by a lake because water comforts me. Fireflies and miniature galaxies usher in the evening, flickering and flashing.

A few months ago I took a leave of absence from Columbia; now I've lost my job. All that's left is cocaine.

I sit up and plunge my arm through the water. I think about diving in.

LAUREL FIDDLES WITH her fork, cuts into her food but doesn't eat it, lets it get cold. My best friend from college is paying a "surprise" visit from Connecticut. Laurel is a planner, an accountant—surprise is not in her repertoire.

"Why did you come?" I ask. I'm late. I hate being late. My guy is waiting. I watch Laurel's lips move, and I will them to move faster. Hurry the fuck up already.

"How long have we known each other?" she asks, inching the bottle of wine that I've consumed to her side of the table. Laurel has an annoying habit of flipping her hair, and now as I watch her flip to the right, to the left, it takes everything in me not to reach over and pull her hair out.

"I don't know, seven years. Your point?" Gesturing at my empty wineglass, I signal for a refill. If I have to endure this, I need sedation. Something to drown out her voice. Because bottle one is merely warm-up; I can still hear each sigh and awkward breath clearly.

"I'm telling you that you scare me," she says. "I let it go at first because I thought it was a weekend thing."

"I imagine one day you'll get to the point." Her voice sets my teeth on edge.

"But it went from a middle-of-the-week thing to a daily fix. Look at yourself, Felicia. You don't look good."

"And she's come down from her Connecticut pulpit to save us all," I say.

"Make me understand," she says wearily.

"There's nothing *to* understand, Laurel. I think you're overreacting. I'm fine."

"You can't even get through a fucking meal without going to the bathroom. No, that's not fine. At least not by my definition of it."

"Is this what we call intervention? I thought there would be more people than this. I must be unpopular, I must be unloved." I snicker.

"Unloved? I guess that's what you would think. Everyone's been talking, our friends have been looking, and they don't like what they see. And they called *me* to talk to *you* because they are tired. They're tired of pulling you back when you've decided, once again, to run out into the middle of the street, or do coke, business, party favors, whatever you're calling it now, with that dealer of yours in a church, that guy, what's his name, rolls up in a limo with a stuffed fucking cat riding in the passenger seat. Or maybe that other time you fell down a flight of stairs, or that other time you tried to kiss your father's girlfriend, or maybe — "

"I don't need another mother."

"And we, *I*, don't want to be one," she replies coldly.

"I'm not like you," I say.

"I'm not asking you to be me."

"Aren't you, though? You don't even know me now. Where were you the past four years when I needed you? I'll tell you where you were: in *Connecticut,* in an apartment paid for by your parents, swimming in your little pool. *You* left *me*."

"I went to business school, I didn't leave you," Laurel says.

"Are we done here?"

Laurel's eyes well, her chest heaves. But still I don't care.

"You're right. I don't know you," she says.

"Stop with the drama. Even in college, you were melodramatic," I say. "Are we done here?"

"You're losing me," she says.

"Then go."

When she leaves, I shut my eyes. Calculating how quickly I can catch the subway to meet my guy in Brooklyn: How soon can I lose this time, this memory, logged but already fading?

"DID YOU EVER have something you wanted to erase?"

"What? What are you talking about?" Merritt asks, bewildered.

"Nothing," I say, flushing the toilet for the third time in a span of a minute. It's our ritual to shield the fact that two girls are locked in a bathroom stall, cutting up cocaine. Every so often, when we need a bump, we take turns—she cuts, I flush. As if everyone didn't know what we are doing.

"There are rocks everywhere. Here, let me do it," Merritt says, carelessly grinding pellets with my Columbia ID card. We've had countless glasses of wine and we can barely make out the bag or its contents.

In the cab downtown, Merritt and I roll up bills, shove them in the bag, and take large sniffs.

I clutch my chest. Something's wrong. Merritt prattles on, but all I can hear is my heart thumping against the weight of one hundred bodies on my chest. I can hardly breathe. When I inhale it reminds me of being underwater, swallowing mouthfuls. The wincing, the insufferable pain—I press on my temples. Breathe, I beg myself, but I can't.

"I can't breathe," I gasp.

Merritt rolls her eyes. "Deep inhales, like in yoga, baby."

"I'm fucking serious, Merritt." At that moment it is entirely possible that my heart could explode through my shirt, shatter the glass divider, and land on the cab driver's lap. It is possible to die.

All color drains from my face and my lips tremble white. Merritt tosses a twenty onto the front seat, drags me out of the car. On the corner of Avenue A, we crouch in the gutter and Merritt makes me throw up, plunging two fingers down my throat. Because what else do you do? Acid lemonade from lunch scalds my tongue. Merritt runs into a bodega and comes back with a bottled water.

"Drink," she says. "You okay?"

I shake my head. People are milling up and down the street, unfazed; they've seen drunks before. They print out receipts from ATMs; they negotiate five friends into a cab when the law allows no more than four; they bar crawl or they crash apartment parties on Avenue A. Everyone's got a plan.

I drink. I focus on being normal, on how simple it was to take in breath and exhale it, before the cab, the uncut coke.

Now, just ten minutes later, we're a street scene: Merritt flying back and forth with water bottles, and me throwing them up. But finally, the breath returns.

Merritt lifts me up; she searches my face for signs of life. "You okay?" she repeats.

I look up at her. "Define *okay*."

Part Two

Black Magic
BROOKLYN 1986

When my mother was a teenager, she practiced black magic. She claimed she placed spells on people, tied yarn around plastic dolls, and, with a small incantation, the victim experienced shortness of breath and the feeling of being strangled. There are so many ways to torture people: sawing off limbs, shredding flesh with a metal cat's paw, passing them through meat grinders—medieval acts performed in basements and makeshift shacks under bridges and expressways. However, it was more satisfying, my mother declared, when you were a shaman. You could inflict pain from the confines of your bedroom. It was discreet, odorless, and untraceable. My mother proudly recounted stories about the people she'd maimed and others who had suffered at her hand.

"You don't know what I can do."

THE PAST FEW WINTERS had been dark, long, and unbearably cold. People bustled along the streets in goose-down coats, with ski masks covering every inch of face, picking up milk, cashing checks, and spending a few moments at the bodega on the corner of Forty-fourth and Fort Hamilton, sipping hot coffee, thumbing through the *Daily News,* mumbling "Wassup." After vibrant steamy summers—with streets flooded from illegally wrenched Johnny pumps, the skin of our backs showing through our white T-shirts, sunburned limbs playing freeze tag in the middle of the street, arrogant yelling at passing cars, bicycles leaning against the sides of trees with the rubber foot of a kickstand scratched from use—Boro Park in the winter became a barren place.

LAST OCTOBER AVI painted all the windows shut. We lived where the air couldn't get in, and at night I boiled from the steam that rose through the radiators. Sweat drenched my blankets. I tried lifting either of the two windows of my bedroom just a crack, but I was locked in, trapped. Mornings I'd wake at five and watch cooking shows or black-and-white World War II footage on Channel 13. My mother left for work at six, and fifteen minutes later I'd slip out and walk the two blocks to my grade school.

I was now midway through sixth grade at P.S. 131, an elementary school with three floors, a basement, and a grand theater. Over a decade later, it would become a magnet school for the performing and language arts, fostering future generations of actors, writers, and artists. But back then it was simply a sanctuary from my hothouse. More than forty grille-covered windows lined the front of the building, some with shades pulled, others decorated with red crepe hearts sloppily cut, a chubby pink cupid taped on the first-floor arts lounge window. There were two courtyards, one on Forty-third and Fort Hamilton (for kindergarten through third grade), the other on Forty-fourth (fourth through sixth), both outfitted with two rows of silver bars that we used for gymnastic flipping and balance beaming. At recess, though, most kids played handball or tossed balled-up paper at the wire basketball hoop. Boys made a game of kicking the backs of one another's knees, then laughed as their friends buckled and fell. The upper grades gossiped, beat boxed, or styled their hair. I took recess in the cafeteria, and on the rare occasions when I did go out, I flipped on the bars or shared one of my Sweet Valley High paperbacks with my few bookish friends.

It was still dark out: The streetlamps glared on ground that once grew grass and trees that once sprouted thick green leaves. I rushed up the steps and pushed through the double doors. The custodians normally arrived at six and left the doors open. The computer room, which housed twelve Commodore 64 computers, two dot-matrix printers, a television with a Betamax videocassette recorder, all donated to the school, was on the first floor. Most of the time that door was unlocked, too. But who would want to come to school this early?

The lobby had two pews, long wooden benches with backs, the sort one would find in a cathedral. I sat and read one of the six paperbacks I had stuffed into my book bag.

"What're you reading today?" Mr. Hernandez asked, plugging

the cord of the floor waxer into an available socket. Mr. Hernandez spit shined his shoes and carted his lunch in an unwrinkled brown paper bag, and he met your eyes when he spoke.

"*The Iliad*," I said, pausing. "But I don't really get it." Dr. Wasserman, our overzealous language arts teacher, believed we could understand an epic Greek tragedy.

"Sometimes it's nice to live in your head. One thing I learned, never mess with an angry woman. They leave scars. Nothing you got to worry about, though."

When I didn't respond, Mr. Hernandez said, "I'll let you get back to the reading. Be careful, you're not supposed to be here until nine."

Last week Dr. Hollman chose me to recite Robert Frost's "The Road Not Taken" over the loudspeaker during morning announcements. My history teacher snuck me a tortoiseshell bracelet from her summer trip to Hawaii. I was soft-spoken and meek, a small child trusted and fawned over, never the troublemaker. My mother made me swallow my voice, not speak unless spoken to, and so I spent my years in elementary school in a petrified solitude, separate from kids my own age. Whenever I did speak, my voice shocked the other students, whose bombastic shouts echoed through the halls, their voices hailing down the stairwells — "Yo, Money! You got fifty cents?" The rare instances when I was called on, the classroom grew quiet and over a dozen heads turned in curiosity. Perhaps they thought I was mute. But my shyness seemed to draw teachers and guidance counselors closer — I was the pet project, an object to be constantly tended, saved.

MY MOTHER WAS a screamer. She was all crescendo. Even in her sleep she was a woman who had to be heard. In our house, there was only one voice: hers. At night she often padlocked her door shut, and I'd often wake to her cries. Once, I crouched outside her door, but all I could decipher was her pleading "Stop," her begging "No," her crying "Please don't leave me." These episodes were like a storm, breaking with ferocity and passing swiftly. One night she forgot to lock the door, and as I inched my way in, I could see her face pressed against the pillow, her mouth gaping wide. There was something so fragile about her face, that velvety Noxzema skin, the way she nibbled on her bottom lip, weedy brows knitted in; she bore no resemblance to the woman who spouted threats, who always reminded you that you were never safe. And for a brief moment I wanted to draw her close to me.

I stood over her, one hand frozen above her sleeping body because it would have been cruel to interrupt her private space, and then I thought of waking her and wondered which of the two actions would be less cruel.

AT FIRST WE called her Ursula. Later we would call her witch, devil, *puta*. When I first met Ursula, she tipped her plate of chicken nuggets and fries all over the basement cafeteria floor; she was known to me as that strange girl who always walked into walls and tripped over her tied shoelaces. At five foot ten, she was the tallest girl in the sixth grade, towering over the boys, who were just sprouting, their voices squeaking into bass. That afternoon when Ursula crept down to scoop up her lunch, she repeatedly banged her head under the table dotted with hardened chewing gum. Exposed pipes ran hissing along the ceiling. It was a clammy, dark place illuminated by fluorescent lights, where we sat on cold metal benches at long rows of tables and suffered the daily stink of hot oil, souring meat byproducts, and boiled unidentifiable green vegetables slung onto plastic trays.

"What's that smell? You guys smell that?" taunted Greg, who proclaimed himself "Greg the Great" and flashed his cap tooth to anyone who would pay attention. Poising his sneaker right about Ursula's rear, he initiated a kicking motion but immediately cowered when she surfaced from underneath the table.

Ursula and I were both outcasts. I slid my brown bag toward her and offered her my lunch. She regarded me, and the contents of my lunch, with suspicion. I'd never seen eyes so black.

"My mother packs my lunch," I said.

Ursula leaned in and sniffed my thermos. "What d'you got?"

I stared at the soggy brown fries accompanied with the lukewarm fried nuggets and offered her half my Chef Boyardee ravioli, some chocolate chip cookies, and a container of Sunny Delight. Mesmerized, I watched as she inhaled the pillows of cheese and beef, as if this were the first time she'd eaten in weeks.

She wiped her mouth with the back of her hand and brushed my shoulder with her other hand, allowing her fingers to linger. "That was *good*," she said.

On the playground she pirouetted around me, but she was Ursula, awkward, large, and clumsy, so her ballet morphed into a ring around the rosie on amphetamines. She circled me in a quick sprint; her thick black hair flew upward in turrets.

"Why do they call you Ursula?" I shouted. "Is that your real name?"

"You know what it's like to be invisible?" Ursula asked. "To be here, but not really?"

Stomping on the pavement, one foot came crashing down and then the other. And it seemed as if she was trying to affirm her existence, to declare this square piece of pavement her real estate. *Mine, all mine.*

"Yes, I do," I whispered, but she couldn't hear me. *I do, I do, I do. You don't know how much I do.* I closed my eyes while she ran wild. Faster and faster she went, preparing for flight. I felt safe.

One day after class Dr. Hollman called me aside. "Maybe it's not such a good idea to hang around Ursula so much. To have only one friend."

"No one wants to be my friend," I said. "I'm too weird, too white, or not white enough. And what's wrong with Ursula?"

"Let's just say Ursula's different from the other children. At her other school, before she came here, there were stories about her and another girl. They were close, like the two of you. But one day, out of nowhere, they stopped speaking. The girl was frightened whenever Ursula came near her. Ursula was angry and had things done to the girl."

"What things?"

Ursula appeared at the doorway, her eyes narrowed to fine slits. "Ready?"

• • •

"You could sleep over," Ursula said. "My mother could make us *arroz con pollo*. I could do your hair." Ursula fastened her pink barrette into my hair. *Qué linda.*

"My mother won't let me," I said. "She's not big on sleepovers or me leaving the house overnight."

"What is she afraid of?"

"I don't know."

It took two weeks of constant nagging to get my mother to consider a sleepover at Ursula's. She acted as if I'd asked to be shipped off to another country.

"I've never heard of her," my mother said, dismissively, "this *Ursula.*"

"She's in my class, at school."

"The same school where that girl in your class, Anna, that Hungarian slut, went and got herself pregnant?"

"Ursula's not like the other girls," I protested.

"If I had the money, I'd send you to St. Catherine's," my mother said.

"Like the Catholic girls are any better," I mumbled, *with their hiked-up pleated skirts and grating haughtiness.* Everyone in the neighborhood held the private-school kids up to scorn. St. Catherine's girls corrected your grammar, the boys traveled in packs with their navy trousers riding low, ties loose, smoking cigarettes; they were smart-ass twelve year olds who thought they knew better than you did. And then I remembered Dina Kabowski, my neighbor with the coke-bottle glasses, who kept begging to play doctor—"just us girls"; "just a tap kiss"—and was suddenly shipped off to Montana after being caught with her hand down a girl's pants in the St. Catherine's ground-floor bathroom. Although we public-school kids were cruel to one another, we all tacitly agreed that Catholic-school kids must be despised. Who, we all wondered, rolling our heads, did they think they were?

"And you don't even need friends. You have *me*," my mother replied.

"It's just for one night," I begged. She liked seeing me on my knees. "Only this once."

Sighing extravagantly, she broke down. "Okay, so who's her mother and where does she live?"

After she got off the phone with Lydia, my mother sat quietly on the couch, knitting. Her needles clinked and clinked. That night as I walked by her room, I peered in and saw her gnashing the pillow in her sleep.

URSULA LIVED ON the fourth floor of a five-story walk-up. Thumping beats and Tejano music—Little Joe and Flaco Jimenez—blared from behind doors of neighboring apartments. Ursula's apartment door flew open and her mother held out her arms and kissed me on the lips. She cocked my head this way and that, her grip firm on my chin.

"*Mira*, will you look at the skin," she squealed at Ursula, "So fine, *muy blanca, mi dios*. An angel, not like my daughter, the *mentirosa*."

Ursula bowed her head.

Her mother was so fast, a frenetic mixture of Spanish and English, hands dancing, conjuring. As I stood in her doorway, I nodded and smiled.

When I looked down, I saw small piles of white powder covering the tattered welcome mat.

"What is that?" I asked.

"*Asafétida*. To ward off the evil spirits," her mother said. "We use it in my religion for many things, exorcism, purification, and protection. But there are so many white powders, one must be so careful, *mi niña*. Make sure you step in it before you enter my house."

"My mother practices Santería," Ursula explained, and immediately disappeared into the kitchen. I could hear cabinets slamming, bowls clanging, and the crinkling of plastic bags.

"Excuse my daughter, she is disrespectful," Ursula's mother said. "She hasn't let Christ into her life. *Ella no ha abierto los ojos en cuanto a el.*"

On the floor was a plush scarlet rug that stretched from one end of the room to the other. I removed my shoes and left them by the door. Sweaters, acrylic blankets, T-shirts, and dirty socks covered the floral couch. Cobalt glasses with scarlet lipstick prints, overflowing ashtrays, bowls of rocks, and a deck of playing cards were strewn over the glass coffee table. White sheets served as curtains. Against one wall stood a large icon case with glass doors. Seven feet high, the walnut cabinet displayed swarthy-faced tribal masks with fat lips and dour expressions, crimson and sea-foam beads, a multitude of silver crucifixes, packets of powders and seeds, wax altar candles in red, yellow, and white, and a large portrait of a brown-faced Christ. From the living room I heard the chime of a small grandfather clock. I could feel Lydia's eyes boring into me, and when I turned around she stood uncomfortably still, partially present, her gaze adrift past my shoulder, lost in the thicket of ornaments tucked behind the case.

"For the god Olorun," Lydia said wistfully, "Beautiful, *sí*?"

I felt disoriented, confused, I was all clammy hands and cotton mouth; but then Ursula reappeared from the kitchen, balancing a bowl of buttered popcorn and bags of Cheese Doodles.

"Mom, *Facts of Life* is on," Ursula said.

Entranced, Lydia clapped her hands and smiled. "Yes, you girls watch the television and I make the lentils."

"*Arroz con pollo,* mom, I promised her *arroz con pollo.*"

Ursula's mother smiled, retreated into her bedroom, and sat at her vanity, mumbling to herself before a marble bust of Christ. She laced rosary beads between her fingers in a cat's cradle. When she was done praying, she drifted into the kitchen.

"Ignore her," Ursula instructed, her face growing hot and pink. "She gets weird like that sometimes. Out of nowhere."

We sat on the couch, bopping to the show's opening credits. Crushed coriander, thyme, and cumin wafted in from the kitchen. I watched Lydia marinate chicken, oil, and seasonings in a large bowl. I got up and wandered into the kitchen. Ursula's eyes remained on the black-and-white television set. The hiss and spit of the frying pan made me hungry. Lydia prepared *pinchos*— appetizers—hot sausage nestled in a bed of fried onions and green bell peppers. To the chicken marinade, she added paprika, Worcestershire sauce, lime juice, flour, and salt.

"I'm making *chicharrones de pollo* instead. You'll like it. Fried chicken in brown beans and rice—but done my way."

Night fell. The windows shined black, and reflections from the street beamed across the television screen. From my perch in the kitchen I could hear *Facts of Life* turn into *Family Ties,* which dovetailed to reruns of *Small Wonder.* The channels kept changing. Ursula's body slackened, easing further down the couch to land on the floor. "I'm still here," she said, sulking.

Lydia cut strips of green banana and dipped them into the hot oil for *fritos verdes.* Frying the chicken in a different pan, she used one hand to tend the thickening rice.

"Tell me, how is my Ursula?" she asked.

I shrugged. "What do you mean?"

Lydia nodded. "I worry about *mi hija,* her heart is so cold. But I know it will get better, I'm praying that she'll open her eyes to Him soon, I light candles, make offerings. Soon she'll forget all about her father. I know this."

Ursula never mentioned a father. This didn't surprise me: So many bastard children where we lived; we accepted the fact that men left, disappeared without a trace, never to return. But Ursula had interrogated me about my parents, became obsessed with my mother, the midnight hospital trips and our chaffings with local thugs and drug dealers. She pumped me for information about my father, the man who disappeared the day after I was born.

"Rosina is your mother's name, right? What is she like?" Lydia asked.

I wondered how to answer such a seemingly simple question. How do I encapsulate the whole of her into a sentence? It might have been easier to tell Lydia exactly what my mother *wasn't* like, but instead I blurted out, "She loves crossword puzzles. Collects them, all kinds." My mother never cared much for books; she would leave them for me — "You're the writer, but remember, I'm your author." However, she voraciously consumed stacks of cheap crossword-puzzle magazines, spent hours inserting words in square boxes in her neat penmanship. I wondered about a woman who had such an arsenal of vocabulary yet seldom used it.

"I see," Lydia said, as if she understood everything. "A woman always seeking answers."

But *I* didn't see, I didn't understand.

When the chicken turned crisp and golden, Lydia mixed in tomato sauce and the creamy rice. The flavors appeared before me, rich and satiny, thick and liquid. Its aroma streamed through the air.

After dinner, Lydia drew a bath. Ursula pulled me into her bedroom. "You're with me, okay? Not my mother."

"What?"

With the water running, Lydia shouted, "Hurry up, *niñas*, before it gets cold!"

Turning to Ursula, I hesitated. "We're taking a bath . . . together?"

"So what?"

Inside the cramped bathroom, steam ribboned, clouding the mirrors and windows. Ursula's mother was dousing the water with blue crystals, humming as she poured.

Ursula removed her socks, unbuckled her belt, and slid her jeans to the floor. Standing there, completely dressed, I was momentarily terrified. I was a private girl—no one aside from my mother had ever seen me naked, and I preferred it that way. And here was Ursula, now completely nude, with full breasts and a thatch of pubic hair, fleshy brown thighs and unclipped toenails. It was too much Ursula all at once.

"Why are your clothes still on?" Lydia scolded as Ursula eased herself into the water.

"I don't think my mother would like this," I said, uneasy.

"What? Your mother don't like you clean?"

"No, not that . . ."

Ursula rolled her eyes. "Then what?"

Moments later, immersed, I drew my knees into my chest. We were quiet and then Ursula splashed me with water.

"Be my best friend," she said. I couldn't tell whether this was a request or an order, but I warmed nonetheless. I didn't have any *real* friends—save for the motley crew of discarded kids clinging together, grateful that come lunchtime we wouldn't eat alone, for that was criminal—let alone best friends. Ursula stretched her legs, settling them on either side of my hips. I concentrated on her face, honey colored and scattered with beauty marks. She had plump lips, small ears, and dark circles under her eyes. She was remarkably ugly.

Splashing her back, I said, "Sure."

"I think Rene's going with Paulo," Ursula said. Our skin had pruned.

"You think?" I asked, trying to hide my desperation but failing miserably.

"She's made out with every other boy in our grade. He's the only one left."

"I thought he wasn't into her," I said.

"You don't have to like someone to fuck them."

"Rene DiMartino has sex? She just has it?" At eleven, I barely knew the logistics of sex, but I did know that sex got you pregnant and it wasn't something you should be doing until you were eighteen — at least that was the talk my mother gave me after she found me with one of her John Holmes movies.

Ursula rolled her eyes. "Who isn't?"

I was devastated. Rene DiMartino was not only going with The Cutest Boy in School, she was sleeping with him, too. Not that Paulo even considered my existence (although he once barked at me in the hall), but out of all the girls, why did he have to date *her*?

"Do you want to try it?" Ursula said. Coming closer, she planted her hands on my knees, knocking them into each other.

Confused, I thought of Dina Kabowski. "But you're not a boy."

"I don't need to be." She smiled, revealing crooked front teeth.

And there was something about that tense moment between her last action and her next that made my stomach cave in. I wound myself into a terrified ball, thinking of unwanted love: Eddie advancing toward me from behind a beaded curtain, all those twinkling plastic shards crashing together, and me opening my mouth to scream *No* but only stale breath coming out. Later, on his bed, he lay spread-eagle and piled new clothes with the tags still on between his legs; he arranged stuffed animals and dolls at the foot of his bed. "I have all these gifts for you," he'd said. "But what, Felicia, do you have for me?" When I tried to scream, his body smothered me, his mouth swallowed mine. *Don't make a sound.* When I tried to break free, he grabbed my arm, twisting it. From the side of the bed, I felt my arm breaking. "You can't leave, pretty girl." And I remembered that day in September when our suitcases were packed and lined up by the door. That was the first time I realized fleeing was possible.

In those few minutes of silence, of hearing dishes being cleaned and toweled dry and Lydia sitting down again, massaging her rosary beads, Ursula inched toward me, her back sloping, and kissed the bridge of my nose. Her lower lip trembled. When I said nothing, she touched the skin above my lip with her tongue and devoured me, proceeding to lick my lips and darting her tongue between them like a determined lizard. The lower half of my face was covered in saliva. Even clean she looked dirty, feral. I pushed her away, shielded my face with my forearms. Although I never had a best friend, I knew this wasn't what friends did.

"No!" I shouted, loud enough for Lydia to hear me, and scrambled out of the tub.

I stood in the hallway, covering myself with my hands. Water dripped on the hardwood floor. Shampoo stung my eyes. Lydia glanced up from her altar, her hands joined together in prayer, and bowed her head before me. She turned away and blew out all the candles, one by one, and the apartment faded to black except for the stark outline of her figure, a white lace shawl wrapped tightly around her neck, and a slice of yellow light from under the bathroom door where Ursula lapped dirty water. *Sucia.*

Lydia tiptoed up beside me and swathed me in her shawl, blanketing me with apologies and explanations. "You must understand. It's so hard for her, *hija.* It's so hard."

I heard Ursula furiously splashing bathwater behind the bathroom door.

THE ROOM WAS MELTING, dissolving into the ground like a Dali painting, revealing a midnight windowless sky: ravens soaring, their onyx wings stretched wide. I gasped, woke up coughing. I couldn't breathe; I felt my neck for ropes, or strings or an extension cord—had something been there, only just unwound?

Voices murmuring. Collaborating. Everything blurry. Echoing. My entire mattress soaked, damp curls tapering around my neck. Was that Ursula darting between rooms, in a copper flowing gown, face covered with scales, wild hair?

And I thought I heard her hiss, "You *will* love me."

IN THE MORNING there were ketchup and eggs, charred toast and pats of butter. The shades were pulled up and light blasted in. A soprano wove through the rooms, her voice soothing, melodic.

"Tell us, how did you sleep?" Ursula and her mother asked. They exchanged looks, giggled.

"WATCH ME KILL HER," my mother said, after I told her about what had happened. "You just watch."

She laced up her Pumas.

She applied Vaseline to her hair, to her face.

She lit a cigarette.

"With my own two hands," she said.

THE DOOR WAS already open, waiting.

"Ursula, go to you room! *Véte!*"

"Lisa, stay here," my mother ordered.

My mother stormed in, got up in Lydia's face. She was fearless.

"You think you could fuck with us? Your sick daughter raped—"

"Mom, she didn't—"

"Shut up!" she yelled, then faced Lydia. "Let me tell you something, you don't fucking know pain. But you will. I'm going to kick your spic ass all around *your* fucking apartment. Do you hear me?"

"Oh, I hear you fine," Lydia said.

"I didn't *rape* her," Ursula shouted from the kitchen. "I *kissed* her."

"What did I say, Ursula?" Lydia appeared angrier with her daughter than about my mother's spouting threats in her living room. "*Oye! Véte a tu cama, ahora!*"

Lydia shifted her gaze back to my mother. "Go ahead," she said calmly, borderline bored. "Do what you've come to do. I've been expecting you."

"You think you scare me? Witch!"

"I think *you* scare you." Lydia laughed.

My mother lunged at Lydia, grabbed her by the neck, and pushed her into the icon case. Ursula's mother shut her eyes. Glass exploded everywhere; trinkets and masks tumbled onto the floor. Ursula raced out from the bedroom while my mother still held Lydia by the throat. Both women were bleeding. I was frightened of my mother's bulging eyes, Lydia's cut but composed face. My mother shook her. "Fucking say something! Say something!"

The room was church quiet.

My mother stepped back, uneasy. Lydia traced her neck and the red marks my mother had left. Ursula and I stood at opposite ends of the room, and suddenly this all felt incredibly wrong. Maybe the kiss was innocent; perhaps I imagined everything. In my thick coat, I shivered, and an unfamiliar look washed over my mother's face—fear. My mother, who once practiced her dark arts from afar, now stood paralyzed, perhaps feared the woman before her, knew exactly what this woman could do. Or maybe my mother had lied; maybe she had never practiced black magic at all.

"Let's go," she said.

When we stepped into the hallway, Lydia came after us, her bare heels on the carpet, her toes grazing the marble step outside her door.

"There are so many kinds of white powder," she said, her face gleaming, bloodied. "You'll see." And she kicked the door shut.

The Language of Strangers

MANHATTAN 2002

I WATCH *Shabby Chic* on TV and realize I need bedding. I need a whole bedroom decorated with floral sheets and a dust ruffle of lime leaves and pink blossoms. It would give my apartment some life. I bolt out of bed and head over to Soho to charge three hundred dollars, on a credit card that will never be paid off, for a fitted sheet and a flat one and two standard pillowcases from the poplin line. And it's a Saturday, a rare morning that I'm awake, not hungover. Maybe it's because of the toothy smile from the coiffed Brit staring out from the books that festoon the antique side tables painted blush, or perhaps it's easier today to put one foot in front of the other without headache, or perhaps this particular Saturday is filled with so much possibility, that I buy into this momentary lapse of sadness. This beautiful, expensive cotton will right everything. At home, as I tuck the new sheet under the mattress, I stare at the flowers, needing to believe this.

I check messages, hoping my ex, Ben, called. But it's only Cathy confirming drink plans.

A week later I pound mojitos with fresh mint at El Rio Grande. A waitress strides past the all-glass bar, carting frozen margaritas on her right arm and waving with her left to the fraternity-boys-turned-suits celebrating someone's birthday. Jocular pats on the back from one gray Brooks Brothers to another. Nicole is busy doling out her personalized business cards, while Cathy adjusts her suit jacket, wondering aloud if a size 6 is considered too fat. I consider appetizers. Buffalo chicken wings drenched in blue cheese. Fried mozzarella sticks lathered in plum tomato sauce.

"You can't be serious," Cathy says. After a brief pause, she wavers. "But I'll nab the celery if you order hot wings. Splurge on a little dressing. Or maybe not. I don't know. What do you think?" Cathy forever worries that she's not trim enough or whether people can tell that she buys knockoff handbags. I want to tell Cathy that none of it matters. Eat the damn wing. But that's Cathy; she has to squint at things.

"Live a little," Nicole says. For the next twenty minutes, she stresses over her unemployment situation and the flailing economy. She blames Bush, she blames a post-9/11 economy, she blames her headhunter—everyone but she is at fault because she still can't manage to find a job. We both worked at and got fired from the failed Italian dot-com that sold designer accessories, but it's been over a year since then and Nicole still can't secure a job. Patting her cashmere shawl, she turns to me. "Remember this? Remember the Cambridge lunches, the town cars? All the money I made? It's downright criminal."

I have a job now, and I suspect Nicole hates me for it. I signal the bartender, who has expertly dodged us for the past hour, for a direly needed refill.

"Slow down. We have to meet the Yale people at Essex," Nicole says.

"Why this torture?" I ask. "What did I do to deserve a night with the Yale people?" The Yale crew consists of rich kids who live in Brooklyn, claiming to be artists. Traveling in packs, they don couture eyewear and Prada loafers, talk up Samuel Beckett as if he is the second coming. Whenever I see them, inevitably someone asks, "Remind me, where is Fordham University?" All I want to do is staple things to their heads. Ben graduated from Yale.

"It's just drinks, Felicia, not the gas chamber," Nicole snaps.

"You sure about that?" I ask.

"We're going because Steve and his friends will be there." Steve is an editor at *Art Forum* and Nicole's husband-to-be. The temperature could break a hundred and Steve would still troll bars in a herringbone sport coat and khakis.

"Someone please give me a gun and end my misery," I say. I pull at sweater threads. They'll all be sober or they'll hold their liquor well. Articulate and well-informed, they'll wax political in their smart outfits and exclude me from their conversation.

I wonder how to negotiate another cocktail order without appearing desperate.

Nicole says, "Can I be honest? Your negative attitude is really not amusing. In fact—"

"It's downright unbearable. You delivered this speech last week, but I assure you it's lost none of its charm," I say.

Before we head downtown, Cathy orders shots and I order another round for good measure.

At Essex Ben is surrounded by all his guy friends, merchant bankers, the ones who tolerated me during our yearlong relationship. When Ben and I broke up, they took him out to a strip club to celebrate his liberation. I also heard he took one of the strippers home, to our bed, the bed we purchased together, the bed that he negotiated in the breakup. I left in a rented moving van with the entertainment center and two bookcases.

"I can't believe I was going to go Jewish for that man," I say, bitterly. "I'm the one who bought the menorah and learned all the prayers."

"Wasn't he self-loathing? He made all those creepy oven jokes," Cathy says.

"You need a man who doesn't have an identity complex," Nicole says.

A collection of glasses covers Ben's table, and he and the boys cozy up to nineteen year olds with epic breasts who are still in college, girls who look like strippers but with better handbags. Ben peers over at me, then whispers in a girl's ear, and she giggles, smoothes his cheek with the back of her palm. I am watching my ex-boyfriend of two months work his way into Barbie's pants.

"We could go," Cathy says. Genuinely sympathetic, she glares at Ben's table. "Look at them," she says. "How low could they go? And isn't Victor *engaged*?"

"They're men bred to cheat," I say. " 'It was just that one girl, that one time,' the rotten bastard said. Right." I tell Cathy and Nicole that it wasn't until I went through his e-mails that I found out about all the women he had slept with, this whole other *life* he had been leading. That "one time" was, in actuality, a four-month relationship. "And he had this whole sob story worked out: He told anyone who would listen that I *made* him fuck other women, that he didn't love them, they were an anesthetic."

"You realize that's a little psycho," Nicole says. "Reading his e-mails."

"And what? Accept that he's telling people that my drinking drove him to cheat?"

"Your drinking *is* a little excessive."

"This coming from the woman who threw up in her bed last week," I say.

"Like you wouldn't do it. Go through someone's e-mails," Cathy says to Nicole. To me, she repeats, "We could go."

"We most certainly *cannot* go," Nicole says. "Felicia, you obviously have to act like you don't care."

"I do care," I say.

"Settle down," Nicole says. "We're with the Yale crew."

"*Nicole,*" Cathy squawks in disbelief. "This is our friend here."

"Don't worry, I won't make a scene," I say. Instead, over the course of the next few hours, I make seven trips to the bathroom, for which I blame red wine and Ben, but the Yale crew doesn't buy it: My table forms a huddle and whispers about my pink nose, the grinding teeth. *Who takes her purse to the bathroom every time?* What follows are the jackets, the wallets, the division of the check nine ways.

Through a tall glass of water, I see Nicole's distorted mouth. "Everyone's leaving," she says. I scour the bar for Cathy, and Nicole sighs and says, "She left an hour ago. You gave her cab money, or don't you remember?"

"Where's Ben?" I ask.

"He went home with some girl," she says. "Ten minutes after we got here."

"Which one?" I laugh, hiccupping.

"We're going home now," Nicole says, in that condescending mother voice I've grown to hate.

Then: the scraping of chairs, the scarves wrapped around necks, terse good-byes.

WHERE ARE THE DAMN KEYS? I lean against the door, frantically rummaging through my purse. Not again. This would be the third time this week I've woken the super. My hair smells of tequila and cigarette smoke from falling asleep at the bar. Which one, I can't remember. What I do recall are voices announcing last call, a wet mop slapping the floor, the chink of loose change in my pocket. Someone who didn't have a car asked me if I wanted a "ride." Heels wobbling on cobblestone streets, I hailed a taxi.

Outside my apartment door, I close my eyes, remembering how I used to watch Ben sleep, his skin fragrant with that French cologne he used. In the bed we bought, he looked so peaceful, child-like; this was a man who loved only *me,* I thought. This was before that night when we walked side by side, taking swigs from a flask filled with scotch, when we both realized that we were drinking to get away from each other; the pavement had widened between us. We drank all the way home. As I fall deeper into sleep, I see my mother's hair and me getting lost in it. "You're safe with me, baby," she says.

Tomorrow is my birthday.

ALONE WITH TWO BOTTLES of wine and a plateful of Tandoori chicken, it's just another day. Another year passing. The loneliness becomes palpable when I flip through dozens of pages in my phone book, scanning names and addresses, finding no one I can call, no one I know well enough to share my day. It's a book of drinking buddies, acquaintances—people I've met randomly. Even Merritt, whom I haven't seen in months, stopped returning my phone calls. Later I page my dealer, Eric, for a few grams. Before he hangs up, he offers to cook me dinner, chicken in that butter sauce I like, or maybe one of those cakes out of a box, with butter icing. I lie. I say my friends are taking me out for filet mignon and brandy.

I even play the part when Eric arrives and hugs me tight; I greet him in chandelier earrings, berry-mouthed. "Damn," he says, "you put the kitty back in cat." I meow.

When he leaves I cut fat lines and hum "Happy Birthday," bit-ing the insides of my cheeks. I wonder if the girl he took home stayed the night, if Ben fixed her breakfast, combed her hair with his fingers when they woke. If they had morning sex. If she was still there.

ALL DAY MY BED serves as refuge from daylight. Medi-cine for hangover. I discover the best place for my head is in the freezer — anything to stop the pressure and the pounding. On the toilet I hold my head in my hands. Peering between my legs, I watch the clear water, and it comforts me until drops of blood sprinkle my inner thigh. In the evening, my stomach is ready to tackle toast.

The phone rings. I cradle the pillow.

"This is Joel. We met last week." The voice is hesitant but con-tinues, "At Guernica. . . . God, is that a cliché or what? I was searching for the best first-call opener, but I'm fumbling here." He chuckles. Again he pauses. "I was thinking maybe we could grab a bite to eat? Or maybe something low-key? Well, I'm here, in my apartment, and this is my number. . . ."

I consider picking up — there's something about that voice, so nervous but earnest, honest, and I rack my brain in an effort to re-member him among the rebound men. Over the past two months, since the breakup, I've dated men who drink gin in lounges on Av-enue B, slick suits who sip scotch in expensive hotel bars, and boys in baseball hats who chug Sam Adams on the Upper East Side.

Was he the one with the bull cuff links? The slacks and button-down? He could be anyone.

When Joel hangs up, I crawl under the covers.

OUTSIDE MY WINDOW, I see a couple on the fire escape one floor below with blankets sliding off their backs. Glass beads drape the girl's neck. She wears her hair teased out, and her boyfriend has cornrows. My building overflows with men hobbling on walkers, women with tufts of white hair as thick as cotton candy, cooing at their miniature poodles—this couple and their nuzzling don't belong to this building. But they keep kissing on an evening that is unnaturally warm for winter. I imagine that they feed each other greasy noodles out of cartons with chopsticks in Union Square Park. Summers, they run through the park, steal blooms from the back of family-owned trucks, and serenade each other in the grass with the flowers in their teeth. They are public with their love. At night they toe wrestle and crank call their neighbors. Burnt sugar perfumes their apartment. They like getting their hands dirty.

I watch their bodies come together, take up lovemaking like cross-stitch, moaning in each other's mouths. And I am afraid I'll never know this love again; never hold it between two fingers, because I'm busy letting myself slip away from myself. From a distance, love seems entirely too hard, always a mopping up, a sweeping down. Who you are is never enough. You need a catch phrase, a story that makes everyone laugh. How would Ben have fallen in love with me otherwise?

LAST YEAR, AT NIGHT, I slept on top of the goose-down comforter Ben bought; I never grew relaxed enough to disturb the sheets. My leg hung off the bed, poised to flee at any moment. One morning I peered over at him—his lips parted, flakes of dried skin on the sides of his mouth—and wondered how he felt safe. Hours later, after yet another argument, he called out to me, sheet wrapped around himself. He wanted to make up, but I was tired. I couldn't speak. I couldn't meet him halfway. He repeated my name, his voice ballooning while I hid in the bathroom, door closed, feeling sonnet small. I kept thinking this was too much.

"Something needs to give," he pleaded. And this frightened me because I didn't know how to be other than how I was.

I hoarded photos—playful images of Ben and me tanned and laughing. We were once our own postcards. We used to disagree over silly things: What we'd name our child, Margot or Lucy for a girl, Ian for a boy. Did we want a teacup wedding or two golden bodies on a beach? Soon enough the disagreements turned into arguments, shouting matches in taxicabs in the middle of Times Square. The drinking was too much for him to bear. He was tired of my going off the coke and going back on again. He told me the drinking needed to stop.

"I drink as much as our friends do," I said. "I don't have a problem."

"Our friends don't run under the Brooklyn Bridge to look for cocaine after drinking two bottles of wine," he replied, evenly. Once, Ben had to physically restrain me from escaping out of a cab; I had been drinking and I was all dried up, my dealer and his son in fucking Disney World; I had practically kicked Ben so he'd let me go. He told the driver to lock all the doors. Ben said I told him horrible things, words he couldn't repeat, and that I'd made him cry, again. "I don't remember any of it," I had told him.

"You never do," he said.

The calling every twenty minutes was obsessive. The *where are you? where have you been?* he found exhausting. During our fights I closed my eyes and heard words like *smothering, suffocating, I need space.*

He couldn't leave; I wouldn't allow it. Everyone always leaves.

"But everything is fine, it's just fine," I cried out. "Look at our photographs. In that bad pizza shop in Utah. See, that's love." We had worn black sweaters and wide smiles. But then he reminded me of all the unkind things we said on that trip; our incessant wheedling and cutting remarks. We fought on line waiting for movie tickets, in the restaurant; we threw clothes at each other in the hotel room. He was finally happy, *relieved,* he told me, when I flew home early. In response, I clamped my hands over my ears.

He shook his head. "You're not listening."

I continued to play house, fixing dinners out of Italian cookbooks and rearranging our books just so. I purchased Egyptian towels and new bath mats. When he touched me, though, I recoiled, drew myself to the very edge of our bed. We slept silently, our feet shifting. My body wouldn't join with his. The closeness was too much for me to bear. I loved him cowardly, on paper but not between the sheets. Soon we didn't touch each other at all, and

I was polite, leaving him in our room with the door shut, with his magazines, videotapes, and other women.

And then Ben broke the ceramic mug I made for him in the sink and left the shards in the drain for days. When I pressed him about the possibility of Julia as a name, he waved me away, said, "I don't know. It's too soon to tell." Dinners became a clinking and scraping of silverware on plates, awkward coughs and a brief, cold statement about our respective days as if filing police reports. He began to come home late, smelling of scotch and sweat; I feigned sleep.

The day I moved out, he jabbed his finger against my breastbone. "I tried so hard to get in there."

"Where?" I said, "My ribs?"

"I have to go," he said.

Everybody leaves.

Before the movers came, I opened and closed the doors of half-emptied closets, stared at my bulky sweaters, J. Crew roll-necks, and thermal underwear; our living together hadn't survived even a change in season.

Alone in my new apartment, I called him every hour on the hour and let the line ring until finally he picked up and asked, "When will you get it?" I created another woman, one who used mint-flavored floss, used floss at all. A woman who didn't panic over restaurant menus, who didn't inquire as to which plates could be altered, who didn't order everything on the side. I pictured her wearing Ben's Columbia sweatshirt, the sweatshirt I gave him, like a dress, her matchstick legs poking out underneath. He sighed and said, "I left you for me," and he broke me when he said, "The more I looked at you, the less I loved you."

A month later I saw him with a prettier version of me at Blue Water Grill. Huddled over a table, they cracked lobster claws and slurped vermicelli. Never mind that this woman spoke with her hands, gesticulated wildly, just like me. Pay no attention to his wearing the Tiffany cuff links I bought him. It was when he dabbed his napkin in ice water and wiped a bit of sauce from this woman's chin that I bit my lip so hard it bled. I wanted to grab his hand, break every bone in it, and say, "This is only a fraction of how I feel."

Coke was there all along. It held my hand, made me feel omnipotent. Sprinkled sweet powder everywhere I walked. I would never be alone.

THE KISSING COUPLE below my apartment disappear through their window, and a part of me wants to let cocaine go. It's becoming a relationship that owns me rather than my owning it. But it's like an old friend who keeps pestering you, making you feel guilty for not returning phone calls. You've been friends this long. It uses that baby voice, whiny. *You need me to get through today.* Coke is the one thing I can leave and a part of me likes that power, and I sometimes flirt with the prospect of abandonment. But lately I feel I need to stop, for real.

Waving a saltshaker overhead, I watch the grains drop through the air.

• • •

FOUR DAYS, TEN HOURS, four home-burnt chocolate chip cookies, seven glasses of water, me rising from my couch and marching to my room, pacing, to lose time, to pass it by. Four days will turn into five. I pace. I turn on the television; flip through two hundred and fifty cable channels. I pause at *All in the Family* and open the window and yell, "Can't you people fucking understand that Evie, or whatever Archie Bunker's wife's name was, died of cancer! Fucking breast cancer!" Across the air shaft, kids laugh and blast pop music. I slam the window shut on a spider attempting to crawl into the depths of my gritty apartment. I cannot drink, because drinking leads to cocaine and cocaine is leading me nowhere.

"Think, buddy, that by killing you I saved you," I will affirm, confidently, semiconfidently, not confident.

I will rise from my couch again and put the dishes away because normal people put dishes in cabinets when they are dry. My father, Gus, calls. He asks me when I'll return to Columbia from my leave. I will even take the rag draped over the refrigerator handle, the refrigerator that tilts to one side, housing various condiments, stale seltzer, and more burnt cookies, and I will furiously wipe the damp dishes dry. I will open the icebox and close it again. I will not eat more cookies. I will—

Phone rings. It's Cathy. "Did you die and not invite me to the funeral?"

"Alive, but barely," I say.

"Don't let Nicole and that bullshit at Essex with the Yale people get to you," says Cathy. "She's completely self-absorbed. Made a fool of herself in front of Steve. Maybe it was a good thing you were drunk." In a smaller voice, Cathy says, "I'm sorry about Ben. God, he saw you and bolted."

I nod into the phone.

"We're going to Tribeca Grand for cocktails."

I can hang up. I can claim that her phone is dying as phones that go uncharged sometimes do.

Instead I say, "For once, I want to try to exercise self-restraint."

"Since when do you turn down men buying you free drinks?"

"Cathy, I have to go. I have to call you back. I have to watch *All in the Family*—Edith has cancer."

"Edith? Cancer? What?" Click. Dial tone. Receiver is set down. Receiver slips from the cradle.

I hear a busy signal, loud beeping. I am ambivalent. Sound, sober sleep.

WEDNESDAY. SEVEN DAYS, a week, even, without a glass, a taste. Daylight does exist. I sit inside crowded La Giara with my unemployed buddies who do platinum-card lunches. I warn them that I have an hour to get back to work. I'm the only one of us failed dot-com-ers who has secured a new job. Half the people I drink with live on unemployment, the other half on trust funds.

"Can I get a gin and tonic," Matt yells at the waitress, hand covering his cell phone. It is 1:02 P.M.

"I think we need to get a bottle? Red or white?" Cathy beckons the waitress to the table.

"What can I get you guys?" she squeaks. Her white plastic, laminated name tag reads Shelly.

"Diet Coke," I say.

Matt covers his phone. "You are kidding me, right?" He returns to his conversation, "Andy, you have to hear this: Felicia's ordering a Coke. This is totally revolutionary."

"Diet Coke," I say. "Unlike you, I have a job and a lunch hour." I will survive lunch. I will not mass murder my friends with their hardened taco salad shells and I will not bludgeon the perky Shelly with my pink straw.

"I know you hate being set up," Cathy says.

"You're right, I hate being set up," I say.

"Well, as all of you know, I am pseudodating Kevin and we ran into Ryan, his very cute trader friend."

"Not a banker," I say.

"You are so dramatic!" She chuckles, clutching her Dewar's.

"Let me be blunt," Matt says. "Honey, you *so* need to get over Ben. From what I heard, he's still on his quest to fuck his way through the East Village while telling everyone who will listen that you're the psycho alcoholic bitch who broke his heart. Have no sympathy."

"Tact, Matt, *tact*," Cathy says.

"Don't date traders," Matt says.

"The market is completely stabilized," Cathy says.

"If I wanted a market report, I'd watch CNN," I say.

Cathy throws her hands up in defeat. "Okay, *okay*. But it would be the perfect segue from Ben."

I READY MYSELF for the date with Ryan, the trader. Alone in the shower, I remember Ben at the bathroom door, asking to come in. Could he join me? We were going out for dinner with one of his lawyer friends, the one who tried cases in court and always lost. My hair was neatly tucked into a large cotton shower cap, like the one I'm wearing now. I never wanted Ben, or anyone else for that matter, to see my hair wet, the thick curls. The soft-knuckle would turn into persistent knocking and then, "Don't you think it's weird that we live together and we've never shared a bath?" By then I had turned off the spigot and we were still, me in the bathroom, he on the other side. You could hear the strained breathing. I told Ben that I liked showering alone; I needed this solitary space. "It's the hair, isn't it," he said. "I know it's not straight, and it's no big deal." Drying off, I said, "No, of course not."

"Don't be ridiculous," I said.

I grab my keys, shut the lights, and, before I leave for my date, realize Ben was right: To me, it's always been a big deal.

Since everyone in New York is afraid of revealing his or her address due to premature stalking situations, first dates always meet at a bad restaurant. It could never be a good one, somewhere you'd return, because if the date doesn't work out, you might see each other there later. So better a forgettable restaurant no one would actually ever go to. He picks Tutta Pasta, off Bleecker. We greet each other awkwardly at the doorway, which is plastered with laminated outdated Zagat reviews from before the fare took a turn for the worse.

"For a pasta place, they have great steaks," Ryan says, ushering me into the dining area before the coat-check lady can issue our tickets.

As we're being seated I crane my neck to scope out exit routes. I'm not good at first dates—they're job interviews with cocktails. Normally, under the soothing transport of two bottles of wine (one consumed before said date and the other, naturally, split between the two parties during the meal), his voice would have dulled to a low murmur. The overhead lanterns, fitted with bulbs too bright, cast a white glare on my hands. Over the course of drinks and appetizers, Ryan's most fascinating topic of conversation is Ryan. I'm sober and Ryan is exceedingly talkative. But I'm working on my lack of inebriation.

After several glasses of Chardonnay, I wave away the bread plate and the garlic-and-oil accompaniment, which resembles castor oil with a dash of pepper. The waiter continually circles the table, asking whether I'd like to order an entrée. Three glares later, he stomps away, acting as if my decision not to eat is a personal attack. I am thick in the business of sedation. A perfect curve of my lower lip etches the wineglass. Ryan cuts into his veal, fingers massaging the flatware. I consider trying to impersonate a person who would act normal, would conduct easy first-date conversation; however, when I open my mouth, all the wrong words come out. It's easy to be cruel.

I lean over and say, "They kill babies to make that, you know."

"Really." He laughs, opening his mouth wide. Gray morsels lie wet on his tongue.

"This isn't the Discovery Channel."

"I could kill Cathy," he mutters to himself, but audibly enough for me to hear.

"So could I," I say, calling for the waiter.

Ryan tightens his tie. "Try the chicken béarnaise, the pilaf," he begs, "*something*."

Hands shaking, I can barely make out the collection of glasses that surround the one plate on the table. I look past Ryan, to the other tables in the restaurant. Why couldn't I be one of those uncomplicated girls cooing her way through a free dinner? Men call waiters for drinks, entrées, desserts, then checks. Leather holders with credit cards protruding are swiped from tables, closing the deal of dinner. This is how it will always go, men leading nowhere. I miss Ben, the temporary home we made. Looking down at my glass, my eyes fill with tears.

I apologize to Ryan. "I was wrong to do this, waste your time. You should be on a date with someone who wants to be here," I say, rising.

"What just happened? Did I miss something here?" Ryan's glasses slide down to the tip of his nose.

"Let's just end it now," I say, attempting a smile, "before we *both* kill Cathy."

I walk toward Christopher Street because I'm not yet ready to go home. The wind razors my skin; I look up at the black sky, which threatens snow. Buzzed, I stumble a few blocks to Caliente Cab Company, a Mexican tourist haven. Bright lights greet me; bulbs highlight liquor bottles. Shouts, loud dance music, and cocktail waitresses sporting Captain Morgan shirts and pirate caps surround me. I blink in disbelief as Shelly, the waitress from La Giara, stands before me.

"I remember you!" she says in a singsong voice. Shelly's pen rests in her peroxide bun. "What can I get you?" She winks.

"Just water," I say.

Shelly winks again and disappears into a thicket of smoke.

Later, after the water turns into countless glasses of red wine, I barely wince when the liquid burns my stomach.

In my apartment, I collapse facedown on my bed. My weight sinks into the mattress, and as the spinning slowly eases, I widen my arms, grab at my new poplin sheets. They wrinkle in my palms. Clothes are fat balls by the nightstand; tubes of glossy lipstick, half-empty plastic pouches, and credit-card receipts litter the floor like cockroaches. A few matchbooks, with phone numbers scribbled in dull ink, names missing or written so illegibly that it doesn't even matter, are in my purse. Then the sickness. I bolt up but know I can't make it—the bathroom, or even the kitchen, is too far, and within moments red wine stains my white sheets pink. All the blossoms recoil, hiding in their leaves. I strip the bed, run over to the sink with the soiled linens, and scrub them hard with detergent and Brillo pads. Nothing changes.

I don't hear the phone ring. It's only when I hear that voice again that I pause.

"Hey, this isn't your stalker, it's Joel. We met . . . wait . . ." He fumbles. "I already said that in my first message. But listen, I guarantee you that I'm much better in person than over your machine, so call me. I don't know," he says, "something about you was really *cool.*" His voice is sober, hopeful. I don't even know him, but I know this—something needs to change. I dump my last gram down the drain. I am done.

Joel repeats his number, takes his time with each digit.

I rush over, pick up the phone, and say, "I'm here."

Pale House

LONG ISLAND 2003

I IMAGINE THAT HOME could be a place where you can lay your head down, finally, to rest. A farm where hens scatter about, wings flapping this way and that. An estate on which my father works exercising and training thoroughbred horses; my friends call him a whisperer. He lives in a spacious garden home on the property, a house that smells of rich pastry. It's oven warm here and quiet save for the lone owl hidden in the trees and the whinny of horses in the paddock. Gus, who is not my father but whom over the last fifteen years I've come to call my father, keeps the horses warm with insulated blankets. In the evening we bring the mares in: My father shows me how to lead them into the barn; he warns me that the young ones might nip at you, might rear up and kick if you're not careful. He tells me this is how they play.

In January, a month after I toasted my twenty-seventh birthday, three months since I broke up with Ben, we cube cheese, thicken sauce with red wine, and the kitchen is fragrant with basil leaves and sweet sausage and fennel. The aroma from the skillets and boiling pots rises in heady wafts and seeps into the kitchen curtains, into our clothes, even the crocheted blanket in the living room. My father tells me, unabashed, that this pie, my apple pie, is the best he's ever had.

"Let me tell you," he affirms, "I never had better."

I tell Gus about Joel and the two-hour phone conversations and the ten-hour first date.

He smiles. "So, what do you think?"

"He's worth looking into."

The flaky golden crust, the hint of orange zest, cinnamon and ground clove — he tells me again that he loves this pie, homemade things. It reminds him of Ireland, of his home teeming with nine brothers and sisters and of his mother's Yorkshire pudding in the oven. Gus rarely speaks of his childhood, and whenever he says the word *mother* it's tinged with bitterness because he's remembering my mother, the woman who abandoned Gus after seven years and an engagement. The woman who once told me that I was the one thing that prevented her happiness and that she sometimes wished I'd never been born and then faked her own death after I refused to let her attend my college graduation. That was just to spite me. Just to get even.

We toast each other with a glass of red wine and hope that the coming year will be a better one. This holiday we talk less than before of my mother. The conversations seem to thin every year. I can't tell whether this is a good or bad thing. In the past, at night, I'd see him go through old letters. He used to write her long, romantic letters, promising her a way out of her life with Avi. And I suppose she fell for him, or that image of a life that she desperately wanted, because they were engaged within only a few months of meeting, even though she still was, and is, married to Avi. To my knowledge, she never filed for a divorce. Holding the letters in his hand, Gus would look up and say, "I loved her once, before, when she was normal. Or maybe she was never normal. Maybe I didn't even know her. All I ever wanted was to cook dinner and live in a nice house; I wanted a family of my own."

Now my father says, "Let's go for a drive."

Outside I notice that the air is cold here, unlike in the city.

In the car we play Pink Floyd and tell each other the old stories we love, memories that change a little over time. Still, they make us laugh and draw us closer. Our humor is self-deprecating, the joke is always at our own expense—but we laugh anyway. We talk about the first Thanksgiving turkey I cooked. When I unearthed the turkey from the oven, my mother stood in the doorway of her bedroom and watched as my father carved the bird. Suddenly the turkey collapsed inward and smoke rose from its cavity. My mother sighed loudly and slammed the door. We heard the familiar click of the padlock and her yelling, "You sure fucked that one up good!" Gus and I drove to 7-Eleven and bought packages of Stouffer's frozen dinners, and that year we feasted on grilled chicken and macaroni and cheese. Not once did my mother emerge from her bedroom.

Gus jokes about their first date. He gave her pink carnations and then she unexpectedly took him to a motel room where they had sex. She even paid for the room. "Cheapest first date I ever had," he said.

The jokes eventually turn sour. We talk about her rages: the time she threatened to burn down the house while we lay sleeping; the time she hurled Christmas dishes over our heads because we grumbled about the film of grease on the cutlets; and that time she destroyed all of my writing, years of handwritten stories and poems torn up with her hands. And Gus and I talk about our mini escapes, how we always left the house between the hours of three and ten. When she came home from work, she'd race past us and lock herself in her bedroom, to drink canned beer and watch TV until she passed out. During those seven hours, we were frightened of hearing the door unlock, panicked, hoping that she wouldn't come into the living room, where we sat paralyzed and speaking in whispers. We decided we'd go for drives and we wouldn't come home until we knew she was in a deep sleep. Fast-food restaurants became shelters. Gus and I were happiest between those hours, passing time in Pizza Huts and Roy Rogerses. Anyplace besides the bedroom in which she stirred.

After my mother left seven years ago, Gus was confused — she wasn't the woman he met in the Belmont diner years before. "She was like this scared little girl who was always begging 'love me, please don't leave me,'" he said. But then he remembered she had become cold, cruel. She was the one doing the leaving. "She told me about those other men, how Eddie used to beat her, Avi got her hooked on drugs, and I could understand why she left them. But why did she leave me? I was good to her." I said I didn't know.

My father and I hold on to our stories like blankets; we clutch them tight—they shelter us. He drives fast, barreling down Glen Cove Road. We've escaped! Look at us go! His smile is warm, his skin fresh with stubble, and the timbre of his laughter lulls me—I can't remember ever feeling this safe with someone at the wheel. I'm nervous in cars, feet on the floor, ready to shield my face. It's all those accidents, the car accident and the shattered collarbone when I was ten, minor fender benders in the city and with friends in different cities. But with Gus I feel safe. I close my eyes while he drives.

Then my father starts in on his death rant. He does this every holiday, reminding me of his mortality, that he could die any minute.

"When I die, I want to be cremated," he says.

"Could we possibly go one holiday without the death lecture?" I ask, rolling down the window, snapping the button lock shut. Everything in his 1985 Cadillac is manual.

"I'm serious here!" he shouts. "Quit it with the window, you'll catch pneumonia with all that cold air."

"So now we're talking about *my* death," I say. "This is a change of pace." Glancing in the overhead mirror, I examine my lips. There is an immediate need for Chapstick.

My relationship with Gus is based on a certain degree of hysteria. Imagine two hypochondriacs trapped in a room, trying to one-up each other. On occasion, say today, one of us will play the sane person, the voice of reason. Assuring the panicked one, *No, you're not dying and no, that cyst on your forehead is not cancer, the numbness in your foot isn't gangrene.* We embrace these imaginary fears, these invented diseases, so as to skirt the real issue: my ex-mother, Gus's ex-fiancée abandoning us.

"Are you hearing me, or what?" His voice booms over the radio station. I sink lower into my seat.

"It's hard not to," I say.

"I don't think you're taking me seriously," he complains. "You don't care. I could die right now. I could have cancer; prostate cancer is huge right now."

"Tell me you haven't been on the Internet again," I say. Gus looks so alive—bright eyes, healthy body, full face—compared to my gaunt figure, whittled down to a size zero.

"I'm serious, Lisa."

Gus squints at the road ahead of him. My father is against buying anything that might reveal that he's aging. For a moment I stare at him, inspecting his tattered jeans stained with paint, oil, and manure, his blunt fingernails blackened by soil, hands callused and strong, arms hairy, muscles defined. He smells of nutmeg, hay, and old sweaters whose stains he's proud of. Every mark from breaking yearlings is its own story. And when I stare at my expensive jeans and $700 handbag, I feel small. I'm hungover and I wonder if he can smell the drinks.

For a while we pretend we are lost, then miraculously find ourselves at home again.

Before we enter the house, my father pauses, and then, "Just once I wish you could come home without a hangover." He tells me it reminds him of nights my mother would leave the house at midnight and wouldn't return until the next afternoon, stinking of liquor, coming down off cocaine. "You don't know what it was really like when you were away at college, how alone I was."

"I've lived with her all my life," I say, "trust me, I know. And besides, I am not my mother." I'm defensive, fuming. He musn't see that my drinking is out of control, that I need at least a bottle of wine to get through my day. That is the one thing I won't allow him to see. I blame my condition on a graduate program from which I've taken a leave, a school where I firmly believe I don't belong. I confide to Gus that everyone had read more, name-dropped dozens of obscure authors they'd recently discovered, and in workshops my stories seemed insignificant, amateur, riddled with faulty syntax and bad grammar. They all talked about finding their *voice* when all I wanted to do was cower and hide. I know they could see right through me.

"There's too much going on," I say. "I just need more sleep. More time to figure things out." What I want to say is this: I'm finally off the coke, so back off. But I don't.

"Don't bullshit me," he says, "I could smell you before you got into the car. Always with the headaches, the damn wine lips."

"I don't know if I can handle it," I say, quietly.

"Handle what?" Gus shakes his head. "With what you've been through, your mother, all of that, you can handle anything. You can't just drop out of your writing program. You have to go back."

"I will," I say, "in the fall." To my father, I'm resilient, steel, impenetrable, and a part of me likes the way I appear to him, so I've been spending the years since Fordham trying to live up to this fiction.

"Sometimes you worry me," he says.

"I'm fine," I say, and I believe this—that I am fine.

"You're in poor form," he says, shaking his head.

Feigning a stomachache, I hide in the bathroom while Gus wipes down countertops and checks e-mail.

After twenty minutes, he knocks on the door. "Tell me, Lisa. What else are you doing?" Cajoling yet another woman out of a locked bathroom; this must be all too familiar to him. Sometimes I find my father staring at me, taking in my hair, the way I pull it into a tight bun, the way I tug at my lower lip when I'm anxious, how quick I am to lash out, and he says, "You're wrong, you're the image of your mother. You're just like her." He says this as if my presence frightens him.

I suspect he believes that I'm becoming her: arrogant, quick-tempered, and fond of living hard. An infectious woman with moxie whose love you grow to regret because it smothers you, wears you down. But by the time you realize this, it's already too late: We've got you boxed in.

We're difficult women, he must think.

My hands can't stop shaking. I taste the inside of my mouth— sour, parched. I fold my hands on my lap and start to count the hours until I get back into the city, to my new Chelsea apartment and the solace of my room and the bottles of red wine in the cabinets.

Over coffee, Gus asks me about Columbia, what I told people when they asked where I was from, about the *we lived in Brooklyn, then here in Long Island, then there, then there.* In response, I shrug and say, "I told people we moved a lot."

"What about when they asked after your family?" He means when they asked about my mother.

I look my father in the eye and say, "I lied. No one needed to know."

He nods and we quickly change topics.

When he falls asleep, I creep outside and wander the farm. The ponds show a thin patch of ice. Hawks circle overhead. Snow begins to dust the frozen ground. Inside the barn, the mares stir; I can hear the foals' snuffling. The children are close, safe. No orphans here. The cats cluster around the old woodstove for warmth. A gray tabby, Nippy, licks her paw.

Before Ben, I called home a three-bedroom apartment with uneven hardwood floors, paper-thin sheetrock walls, that I shared with two strangers who always locked their bedroom doors. We communicated via yellow Post-its. Now I live alone in a building where neighbors blast music and have orgies. I've moved every year since I graduated college, and I'm starting to think that a home is simply the place where my mail is forwarded.

I rest in the tack room, bring my knees up under my chin, and I remain that way until early dawn. Until all the lights go on in the house, until the percolating coffee and the smell of rye toast.

At the train station the following morning, my father waves to me from inside the car. Snow falls in chunks on the windshield.

"We need to put your mother behind us," he says. "We have to forget her."

How do I tell him that forgetting is the thing I want to do most but for some reason I can't.

And for a small moment I want to remain here, but then a part of me wants to leave, and I wonder how long I'll be stuck in the betweens. Which place I could call home.

Desperate Creatures
BROOKLYN 1987

ONCE, MY MOTHER CLAMPED down so hard on my nose, tugging until my shirt was covered with drops of my blood, that I
had to lean my head back, breathe through a wad of toilet paper.
Playing noogies, she called it. Other times she hugged me so hard
it seemed she was trying to bury me in her. I could feel her ribs
against my face and hear her jaw clicking from the spearmint gum
she chewed. She held my head against her chest so tightly that
I couldn't move. And I realized then that my mother could put
me on pause, still my breath if she wanted to. I waved my arms,
shouted into her smock that I couldn't breathe. It was only then
that she let me go.

AT NIGHT MY MOTHER left me alone with Avi, who hid out in the bedroom listening to eight-track tapes of Neil Diamond and Carole King. He ignored the strange men who knocked on the door at all hours to ask if my mother or father was home. Recently we had installed a sliding bar lock in addition to the three dead-bolts and chain locks. We were a family obsessed with security. I yelled that no one was home, that I was alone but the phone was right here next to me, that the police could be here in a minute. But I was only eleven, hardly intimidating. Laughing, the men told me their names, which were never their real names, but "Trust me, your parents know who we are and how much they owe us," they shouted as they descended the stairs.

THREE YEARS EARLIER Avi had moved in, dragging his paint buckets and two nylon suitcases up six flights of stairs. One morning a week after he settled in, when he decided to repaint all our walls, my mother and I rode the train downtown to a nondescript office building where we sat on plastic chairs, waiting for our last name to be called. Hours passed, how many we didn't know because the overhead clock remained fixed at noon or midnight, depending on how you looked at it.

My mother squeezed my hand tight. "Show me sad," she said.

"I am sad," I said.

Our name was called.

"Good. Keep that face for another fifteen minutes."

A fat black woman with wiry hair and spectacles that hung from a braided string reviewed my mother's application for welfare.

"It says here you went to college," the counselor said.

"For a year," my mother paused, "and then I had my daughter."

After a few more questions and a stretch of silence, the counselor leaned over and sighed, "You're kidding me, right? You're *white*."

"What does that mean?" my mother asked, her knee bouncing. Lately her body had become her own roller coaster.

I tried to make the saddest face.

"That means get a job. Any job. Or come back to me when you have a few more kids."

"So what you're telling me is that we won't be getting any money," my mother said. "Not even food stamps."

The counselor met my mother's eyes and then called out, "Johnson, Awilda Johnson."

That night Avi said, "I know some people, Italians." I could hear him talking to my mother through the walls. "They're white like you, they'll lend you the money at a good rate."

"I don't know," my mother said, uneasy. The bed squeaked.

"Let me tell you what I know," Avi said. "Javier doesn't like not being paid."

I could hear cutting. I could hear my mother blowing her nose.

"Here," Avi said, "take the Afrin."

Javier dropped by a week later. In the doorway stood two men in down jackets, silent, arms folded into their chest. My mother gave Javier a small, thick envelope. He kissed my mother on both cheeks and left.

When they closed the door, Avi asked about the Italians. How much had she borrowed, the rate.

"Don't ask me what I had to do," my mother said.

THE WEEK BEFORE, my mother had been fired from yet another diner because money had mysteriously disappeared. Except for the owner, she had been the only one entrusted with keys: *Who else could it be?* they all said. Police were not called, charges were never filed; the owners knew about my mother by then, about her friends, so they let her go quietly with a few weeks' pay and tips. How quickly that money vanished, along with the contents of our refrigerator and the 18-karat gold studs she gave me for my eleventh birthday.

Soon after, Javier was replaced by George, who dropped glassine bags into my mother's coat pocket and always coughed before he spoke. When he heard that my mother had scored a job as a deli manager, he whistled, nodding his head in approval. Through all this, Avi ghosted in the background, reminding my mother that they had to keep working: Their house, their bodies, machines had to keep moving. So he painted and drywalled houses all over Brooklyn, and my mother rose in the early hours, when it was still dark, and, with a quick bump of coke, willed the makeup on and moved her body out the door.

In those days George came by at least once a week. George never touched my mother, never kissed her cheeks.

• • •

ON THE WEEKENDS my mother and I rode the subway into the city. Resting my head on her lap, I stretched my legs long over the seats. The rattling car, the rustling newspapers, the crackling voice announcing each stop, and the goings-on of passersby soothed us. At Lexington Avenue we wove our way through the crowds; my head craned every which way just to *see* everything. Against the towering buildings and magnificently paned glass, I felt incredibly small. To me, Manhattan was horrifying and grand. Tourists planted themselves in the center of the sidewalk, accordion maps opened wide, charting which way to go. We headed west to Park Avenue, to the delicatessen where my mother worked as head manager.

When we arrived at the deli one Saturday morning, I said, "We're home."

My mother threw open the metal gate. "Not *home*, Lisa," she said, puzzled. "This is *work*."

I thought about the times I had gorged on pints of Frusen Glädjé ice cream there and how, at the end of the day, I'd feel giddy, buzzed, and slightly sick. And then I thought of our apartment and our freezer with its lone ice pop covered in burn.

After she keyed in the alarm code, I bolted inside—I couldn't help myself—and marveled over the pristine linoleum floors, at the revolving display of potato chips, pork rinds, and Cracker Jack suspended from metal clips near the door. Boxes of Nerds, stacks of watermelon gum on the racks in front of the register, boxes of pasta and tissues perfectly arranged on the shelves. Cans of Coke, Tab, and Pepsi in gleaming rows behind the clear refrigerator doors at the back of the store.

"We could live here," I said.

"This isn't our home," she said.

From the kitchen in back, my mother and I lifted heavy buffet trays. Adjusting food temperatures, she warned me about how hot or cold food must be in order to serve it. Blisters formed on my arms from the metal and the heat.

"But the chicken's burned," I said, pointing to the caked-on barbeque sauce.

"How it *looks* doesn't matter," she said, "following the rules matters. What the Board of Health says matters." My mother looked proud uttering the words *Board of Health*—how official it must have sounded to her—and I could tell it pleased her that she knew something other than how to balance seven plates on one arm. When you entered our living room, you couldn't miss her certification in food management, in a gold frame, on the coffee table, her name in elegant cursive. And if you moved it to one side, peeked behind, you would see two smaller frames. Pictures of me.

While I rang up items at the register, my mother wrapped tuna melts and roast beef on rye in plastic. When she loaded the last of the prepared sandwiches on a tray, she leaned back against the counter, pulled down a pack of Kents from the overhead cigarette rack, and puffed away. From a register rich with bills, I doled out change and tore off receipts as my mother's boss, Lenny, watched approvingly.

"Hello, pretty girl!" he bellowed, carrying bags of nuts, dried cranberries, apricots, figs, and licorice. He presented the plastic bags as gifts, scattered the bounty on the counter. Eyeing my bag of Fritos, he shook his head and smiled, revealing two gold teeth amid all the white. "Pretty girl shouldn't be eating chips if you want to grow up strong, healthy like your mother," he said.

My mother's face grew dark. "Don't worry about what she eats."

Lenny winked at me, and to my mother he said, "Of course, of course."

Saturday mornings my mother and her boss would review the weekly ledger. Because of her waitress background, she took to numbers easily, and Lenny taught her basic accounting: debits and credits, margins and net profits; how to balance a budget, how to make numbers foot.

"Someday I'll make you partner," he said to my mother as they discussed the day's late deliveries. "When I own *fifty* delis. And I will own them."

"Fifty delis," she mused.

I beamed, chewing on licorice.

Lenny smoothed my hair. "Your mother is a smart woman. She knows the business. Watch her," he said.

And when I asked if I, too, could work in the deli, Lenny laughed and said, "Of course. Who else knows the register so well?"

When he left for the day, satisfied with the work we'd done, my mother held me close. "One day we won't need his money," she whispered. "We'll have our own."

For lunch we'd fix ourselves sandwiches—salami, cheddar cheese, and turkey piled ridiculously high between two slices of white bread, with mountains of iceberg lettuce and juicy tomatoes—and sit on stools in front of the register. Food spilled out of the corners of our mouths. After lunch she'd map out the specials for the week while I brown bagged orders.

"You see my girl, that's my girl," she'd say to customers. "Eleven years old and look how good she handles money. Better than me."

I loved it at the deli. There were no empty fridges, no pinching pennies for cold cuts or lox. And the overhead fluorescent lights glowed in a way that reminded me of sunlight: even when it stormed outside, inside it was calm and warm. Methodically I stacked soup cans on the shelves; I took comfort in aligning the cans just right so their labels faced front, uniform and neat. I stickered boxes of sanitary napkins, Pampers, Dixie cups, and aluminum foil. I shook bags of Skittles and peanut M&Ms like maracas, pretending I was Carmen Miranda with a fruit hat towering over my head. Evenings I helped my mother clean the Employees Only bathroom, filling it with freshly cut carnations and air freshener. It had an endless supply of soft tissue, just the way a home should have—not like ours, with its dingy, yellow toilet, overflowing garbage cans, and mushrooming tiles.

The deli also housed an upstairs office with a desk, an overhead lamp, a few file cabinets, and a floor safe. It was a dim, closet-size room, like a monk's cell. Posters of soup cans, cereal boxes, and 1940s Varga girls covered the walls. Before my mother closed for the night, she'd fiddle with the combination and deposit the day's cash and receipts in the floor. Drowsy, I'd wrap my arms around her waist while she shut off all the lights, locked all the doors. For the past few weeks, my mother had been quietly fixing the books. Handwritten invoices were simple to doctor, and Lenny hardly missed a few twenties here or there because he thought he could trust her. He had given her keys to the store; she knew the combination to the safe. When I saw her forge signatures, heard the dollar bills crumple in her hands, heard her laughing in the bedroom with Avi, I wanted to say something, I wanted to break down the door. But when I opened my mouth, no sound ever came out.

WHEN WE ARRIVED home from the deli, Avi was at the door, waiting for us. "Two men, your connection, came to my job in Bensonhurst," he barked as soon as my mother stepped inside.

"Now they're *my* connection," she said, resting her purse on the table. I slipped quietly into the other room and pretended to fall asleep on the couch.

"They cleared the fucking place out. Came in that black Cadillac. Took the paints, the brushes, the ladders, took it all. *Collateral* the motherfuckers called it. I had to send Luis to Benjamin Moore for more paint."

My mother drummed her fingers on the chair. "A month," she said. "We're only behind a fucking month."

Avi went on about the two men: *We like Rosie,* they said. *We knew her when she was this high,* they said, raising their hands to their knees. *Like one of our own,* they said. *We can't keeping letting this slide,* they said. *One month turns into two. You know how it is.*

"We need your job, Rosie," Avi said. The volume on the television was turned up. "Remember what they did to Cesar after six months, his children in that trunk? His wife half in the shower, half in the kitchen."

"I know," my mother said. "Don't you fucking think I know?"

I slipped into my room and I built a fortress under the bed with my covers and stuffed animals, the bears, the bunnies, and the plush whale—and, of course Big Michelle, my life-size plastic doll. One of her blue eyes had fallen out. I clung to my family, I drew them closer.

ONE NIGHT MY MOTHER knelt on the carpet and clutched my shoulders. Tonight, she announced, I would be in charge.

"Where are you going?" I asked.

"Out with Concetta. You remember her. Make sure you lock all the doors."

I shuffled my feet. My mother was going out with a woman who worked in a day care center and stole televisions. "It's a school night. You have work tomorrow."

She leaned back, sat cross-legged on the carpet. "I know what day of the week it is," she snapped. "All of a sudden you're my mother. I answer to you now—is this the game we're playing?"

"I hate being alone."

"Avi'll be back from Atlantic City tonight," she said, rising.

"He does this all the time. Disappears."

"You think you know everything, don't you?"

I watched her chest rise and fall. She was grinding her teeth. Her jaws clicked.

My mother couldn't stop moving, even for a second. Watching

her, all I needed to do was replace the eye color, darken the skin a few shades, kink the hair, and she would be the image of her sister Marisol, a heroin addict who spent her days in a deep nod when she was high and searching for money to steal when she wasn't. And now the discos, the hair piled high, and the quick sniffs.

Fists clenched, I shouted, "You should know better. And those men who keep coming over? Asking for you, for Avi? What kind of mother leaves her daughter alone?"

My mother pinched my arm so hard I fell to my knees, whimpering.

"Try finding better," she said.

Hours later I woke up. All the lights were on. I crouched low and crawled out of my room, barefoot. Glass table lamps glowed bright, ceiling lights and sixty-watt bulbs illuminated the rooms, giving off the impression of daylight. The front door was wide open—all the locks freed, the windows unbolted. I moved from room to room. Nothing was missing; everything was in its place. Except for a note that read "We liked watching your daughter sleep." I ran into the hall and downstairs to the ground floor. It was so cold. Standing in front of the landlord's door, I wondered whether I should knock, if I would be interrupting their sound sleep. Would that be rude? I rapped on the door anyhow, and the tall woman opened it, still wearing her black pageboy wig. She climbed the flights, hunted through each room, in the closets, under the beds, and assured me in a calm motherly voice, "No one's here. You could come back in."

I lay in bed, stared up at the ceiling. The landlord lingered over my forehead, her lips moist and slightly puckered, but suddenly she retreated. Maybe she was afraid of my mother walking in on us, afraid of what my mother could do.

After the sun came up through the trees, Avi came home. He reached inside the refrigerator and poured himself a glass of buttermilk. His eyes were bloodshot, and from his shirt pocket he unearthed a bottle of Afrin. After a few sniffs, he hacked, cleared his throat, and stared at the loaf of white bread on the table. I continued to eat my cereal.

"Where is she?" Avi asked. He held a slice of bread in his hand and pressed it with his fingers.

"With Concetta."

"All night?"

I nodded.

He sighed, tore the bread into miniature pieces. "She has work today." In a smaller voice, he said, "They've been warning her. About being late. About not coming to work at all."

"Did you come home last night? Early?" I asked.

He paused. "Was someone here?" His voice was hoarse, tinged with fear. "In the *house*?"

"I was here," I said. Rising from the chair, I went over to the sink, turned on the tap, and furiously scrubbed my bowl with a wool pad. Lathered it up with soapy hot water. My fingers tingled from the soaking. But it felt good, necessary.

I felt Avi's eyes on my back.

"You don't need to go at it that hard," he said. "You can use a sponge."

"I know."

Then we heard keys fumbling, the easy slip of metal in and out of the locks. We froze. Without looking at either of us, my mother jetted past, leaving a smell of stale cigarettes and powdered musk in her wake.

Avi folded and unfolded his hands. His wiry hair was flecked with paint. "I have a drywall in Canarsie today. I can drop you on the way," he said to me.

I turned the faucet on full blast to drown out his voice.

"I'll go on my own," I muttered.

JUST AS AVI had predicted, my mother lost her job at the deli. They were closing down, Lenny said. Maybe they would re-open in New Jersey; they didn't know. Avi shook his head and said they really fired her because she was always late, but they were too scared to tell her. The night after she was let go, I awoke to find her in my room.

"Wake up, wake up," she said, shaking me from sleep. Rubbing my eyes, I reached for my eyeglasses on the nightstand. For a few seconds my mother appeared as a soothing blur of black hair framing white. But when she came into focus, she looked haggard, unstable. Her teeth were chattering and a cluster of pimples dotted her chin.

"What's wrong?" I asked.

"We have to go," she said. "Put on your clothes."

"Go *where*? It's the middle of the night." I was scared that she had lost it, that she finally had gone crazy. Because she looked crazy.

"We're meeting Concetta for a thing. A thing. At the day care center where she works. But we've got to go now."

When I didn't say anything, didn't move, my mother stripped the blankets off my bed. "I need you to keep watch for us. We need this money. Don't you understand how much I owe?"

"Not me," I said in a small voice.

"Who else if not you?"

I slid to the floor and drew my knees up close, allowing what she'd said to sink in. Our days at the deli were over. There would be no more gorging on cold cuts and ice cream. No more arranging of the endless rows of treats. After all the months my mother had spent in training, I had really thought this time would be different.

"I'm not going anywhere!" I said, inching myself up. I made a break for the bathroom and hid behind the locked door.

My mother pounded on the door so hard I thought the hinges would break. "Get your ass out here this minute! Wait until you get out of the bathroom. See what I'll do to you." The banging was louder than bombs.

I sat in the tub and clung to the plastic shower curtain with the dancing ducks while she cursed, threatened, and begged. I knew she could break down the door if she wanted to.

Suddenly it was quiet. She was gone.

MY MOTHER DISAPPEARED for a week. Avi and I went about our respective days watching her space on the couch grow cold, the blankets she knitted tossed aside, bits of yarn coming undone. One morning as he dropped me off at school, Avi claimed that it was a good thing, her being gone. "Let her cool off," he said, gripping the steering wheel of the station wagon. "Get her head together."

THE FIRST TIME I met Avi at my mother's diner, his face was covered in bruises the color of ochre. Later I would learn they came from men who were displeased by his unpaid gambling debts. Over breakfast he gave me a sack filled with pennies and said, "Here, this is for you." At the door of the restaurant, he stood waving, the ever-present paint speckles on his hairy arms. My mother smiled. She leaned over the counter, her welts and bruises having finally healed after leaving Eddie, who beat her with his hand when she was good and with belts and tools when she was bad. "That man's going to take us away from Eddie, from Marisol, the drugs. All of it," she'd said. I looked at them both, their bruises and their smiles.

When they married a few months later at City Hall, I wasn't invited.

Barely a few months later, my mother had whittled down to nothingness, all sallow skin and bone. She pushed food around on her plate as if it sickened her to look at it. She'd started to hide vials of coke in her pocketbook, behind the toilet bowl, in the sugar canisters, in my pillowcase. She made a great deal of money from waitressing and stealing from her bosses, but couldn't explain how she spent it; her hands trembled all the time, she grew her pinky nails long, she sought sanctuary in locked bathrooms.

I despised Avi. I loathed his fleshy lips, his brittle mustache, and how he spit when he talked. How he reeked of paint and household cleaning products mixed with body odor. His damn T-shirt that read Avi's Painting—We Do the Best for You. And this is what I hated about him most: He cut my mother her first lines of cocaine.

"I'm late for homeroom," I said to Avi, and headed inside.

A WEEK BEFORE my twelfth birthday, I woke to the smell of buttermilk pancakes and brown butter. I could hear skillets crackling and hissing. I tiptoed into the kitchen to find my mother cooking me an elaborate breakfast. Sugared blueberries, raspberries, and diced bananas spilled out of small glass bowls. Fried sausage links and hotcakes topped with rich maple syrup covered my plate. The abundance of food irked me. We'd been living on thirty-nine-cent packets of Oodles of Noodles for two weeks.

"What's all this?" I asked.

"What does it *look* like? Breakfast. Eat before it gets cold."

"Where are my Lucky Charms?"

"In the garbage," she said, whistling. "Cereal was yesterday. Today we have pancakes."

She sat down and watched me eat. Between forkfuls she smoked Kent 100s down to the filter, and when I was done she collected the plates and piled them up in the sink.

"Get dressed," she said. "I have your gift."

In my room, double knotting my shoelaces, I wondered what my mother wanted from me.

Outside we passed windows displaying narcissus, bulbs exposed, blooming wildly. A carousel of twinkling lights and large-scale nativity figures decorated lawns. Gutter puddles glimmered with ice that hadn't completely frozen. The snow was coming down in sheets and I felt the crunch underfoot.

"Where are we going?" I asked.

"Into the city," she replied, curtly. But first we stopped in front of an abandoned house. Vacant warehouses, dilapidated cars with windows bashed in, sidewalks and storefronts covered in graffiti, "Sharky was here," glass shards from smashed beer bottles, marked the street. The only sound was a Villabate's Bakery delivery truck puttering its way to the crowded thoroughfare of Thirteenth Avenue. The street appeared blighted, with gray buildings and dead weeds. We paused in front of one of the two houses on the block. My mother told me to wait outside, that she would only be a minute.

Planks were nailed over broken windows. I watched her enter through a front door that was missing its knob. I stood in front of the house, shivering and scared, rubbing my hands together, then balling them up inside my coat. It was hailing. After an hour, my mother materialized, glassy-eyed, jittery.

"Let's go," she said, tugging my arm, "we don't have time."

At the subway station, I asked, "What's in the city?"

She was cryptic in her response. "Your gift. I'll tell you on the train."

We boarded the last car of the B train and sat huddled in a two-seater by the conductor's booth. "We're going back to the deli," she said.

I started to shake my head. My mother grabbed me by the chin

THE SKY ISN'T VISIBLE FROM HERE

and said, "Listen to me." Her eyes were so black. The car was empty except for two women yelling at each other in Cantonese, arranging their red plastic bags about their feet.

"I'm listening," I whispered.

"All you need to do is talk for ten minutes. You can do that, right? Be like me. I'll just be in the office collecting what's *mine* . . ." And then my mother's voice trailed off. Talking to herself, she seemed foreign, distant. "They told me they were closing down, they were going bankrupt, but they lied to me. Hired someone else. A woman they could get over on. Could *fuck* with. They think they can get over on me, but I'll show them." Her face was tight. She pounded her thighs with her fists. "And so what if I took a little money? So what? They owe me," she said. "They took my money from me. They took my job from me."

I wondered why my mother couldn't just let it go, why she always had to hold on to her anger.

"We'll be home before you know it."

When we came out of the subway she said, "Keep Lenny busy for ten minutes, okay?"

"What am I supposed to talk to him about?" I said.

"Make something up. Tell him about school. For *Chrissake,* do I have to do all the work here?"

I could tell I was pushing her. She could explode. She would blame me for ruining her plan, for messing everything up.

Inside the deli, the overhead light fixtures, which had once seemed sunny, now seemed too bright, turning the floors and walls hospital white. Fumes of ammonia and bleach hung heavily in the air. The floors were still damp from a mopping. Lenny regarded my mother with suspicion but softened when he saw me. He laid a hand on my head; his fingers were warm and moist, smelling of stale cigarette smoke and cinnamon.

"Little girl, one day you're going to grow big." He chuckled, fluffing my hair.

"She's big enough," my mother said, a toothpick lodged in her teeth. I felt as if I were being passed between them, an object for them to pet, to coddle. She massaged my shoulder, grinning. "I'll only be a minute."

My mother said she had come to collect the rest of her things and get her final paycheck from the office. As soon as she disappeared, I started to talk. I told Lenny about my clarinet and how I could finally play the *Star Wars* score and the national anthem. Can I play for you? I asked him, chattering on when he didn't answer. There was a sense of urgency for my mouth to keep moving, for my words to cover up the goings-on upstairs. As I prattled on, I noticed Lenny eyeing the office door, silently timing my mother. His brows knitted, his jaw tensed.

"Just a second," he said, walking toward the office.

I scanned the store, searching for diversions. A stack of candy that I could accidentally knock over, display cases I could bump against, *anything*—but everything was tucked away, in its place, immaculate and clean. I was torn between wanting to stall Lenny and wanting to expose my mother to him.

Suddenly my mother surfaced, holding up a pair of sneakers, speaking in my stead. "I looked everywhere for them. Imagine

these getting lost. I found them in one of the file drawers," she
said, doe-eyed and breathless.

Lenny took her hand in his and said, "I'm sorry for how things
turned out. Try to understand these things happen."

"I got what I came for," my mother said. "Come on, Lisa, it's
getting late. We have to go."

And with a wave, we left, and a few blocks down, my mother
peeled five twenties from her bag, which overflowed with cash.
"Happy Birthday," she said. In the middle of the street she danced,
swiveling her hips and snapping her fingers to an imaginary beat.

She shoved her head into her black bag and inhaled.

I held the bills in my hand. I was rich! The thievery, the fact that
my mother could get arrested, that I could get sent to a home, fell
by the wayside. All that remained was the money, the great sums
of it, and the fact that she would likely get away with it again.

As we made our way to the subway, I peered at the storefront
windows; the crowded, shabby displays of mannequins modeling
garish heels, pocketbooks hanging from their arms like pendulums,
the torn bean-can labels peeking out from bodega windows . . .
It was overwhelming me. Everything appeared used, sickly. Not
like the *gleaming* deli we had just robbed. I brought my hand up
to my chest; I couldn't breathe. It was only when I let go, a few
twenty-dollar bills fluttering away, that I joined my hand with my
mother's. I reached out for the money but my mother pulled me
back. Didn't I know there would always be more? she asked.

How quickly money goes, how it flies out of your hands before
you remember whether you held all twenties or tens. My fortune

was spent within a few weeks, on sheets of Lisa Frank stickers, feasts in diners, and a midnight blue jumpsuit with silver stars. In middle school I was meek, shy, but now, in junior high school, I was more confident. For weeks I wore the jumpsuit to school, pranced around homeroom, raced down the hall as bits of glitter trailed behind me. *"Qué linda,"* everyone said, fingering the soft cotton. It felt good to be envied.

And after the money was gone, all spent on the items folded neatly into drawers or protected in albums with plastic or consumed and my fingers licked clean, it occurred to me that this was what it felt like to have less than what I started with. The excitement of that day dissolved quietly, swiftly, as my mother lay comatose on the couch, staring at nothing, getting lost in it, while Avi buzzed about the house, making lists of people to call and running out to the pay phone down the street, frantically trying to drum up some business. The week before, AT&T had shut off our phone. I locked myself in my room and lay on the bed, petting all my pretty new things. But as each day passed, these things, which were only things, began to grow old, their luster faded.

FIVE MONTHS LATER, Avi strapped cardboard boxes filled with our possessions, the whole of our lives, onto the top of the station wagon, crammed them into the backseat, filled any space he could find. We were moving to Long Island, starting over, they said. But twenty minutes into our trip, as we barreled down the Brooklyn-Queens Expressway, my mother screamed. The cords had loosened, and boxes tumbled down on either side of the car, spilling their contents. Among the mismatched socks, records, and costume jewelry that poured out, I watched my beautiful blue jumpsuit with the silver stars flying up in the air, soaring amid the traffic, quickly flying away. I wanted to swing open the door or climb out the window after it, but it was already down the road, sliding back toward Brooklyn. Cars swerved, but there were no accidents. We veered onto the shoulder, recovered what we could. Avi tied whatever was left on top of the car as tightly as he could. And as we sped farther away, our old home behind us, a new one ahead, I could barely make out the jumpsuit anymore. It had been a reduced to a glinting speck on the road.

Points of Entry
LONG ISLAND/BRONX 1989–1997

YOU HAD BEEN in chrysalis for as long as you could remember, but by adulthood, you had become an expert at transformation.

Tools:
One round brush
One wide-toothed comb
One curling iron
One flat iron
One tub of Revlon chemical hair-straightening cream
Two blow-dryers
A jar of mayonnaise
Boxes, jars, and tubes of antifrizz products

Two white cotton towels

A bathroom door, locked

Results:

When you were fourteen, your scalp was burning, you left
the cream on for two hours longer than the instructed
forty-five minutes—you desperately needed this product
to work. That night you almost had to go to the emer-
gency room because you were blistering, bleeding, and
screaming.

When you were fifteen, your hair turned orange.

When you were sixteen, your hair fell out in clumps in the
shower.

When you were seventeen, you seriously considered shaving
your head and buying a wig.

All this suffering because you wanted to be like Amy, the dance-
team captain who sat in front of you in biology class.

YOUR MOTHER WAS SLEEPING when the Stern's store manager called. You were in custody, under guard in a room with four
shopping bags filled with slouchy socks, neon hair scrunchies,
black clogs, and piles of shirts, shorts, and bathing suits from the
juniors' section. You walked two miles to Green Acres Mall that
Mother's Day, ready. You went with an arsenal of magazines, dozens of photographs and Polaroids. You would steal all the trendy
clothes and accessories your enemies had hanging in their pink

closets and crammed into drawers. In high school, you entered the homes of your enemies—the cliquey rich kids who snubbed your "last year's" jeans, your makeup-free face, and your frizzy hair; but make no mistake, the poor white trash loathed you, too—and took pictures of their vanity tables, the posters on their walls, and the insides of their closets. In Valley Stream, Long Island, people used to leave their doors unlocked, and you'd slip in during your two free periods, snap photographs, and leave. Your enemies' rooms smelled of that apple shampoo they all used. Sometimes you would linger over a dirty cheerleader sweater turned inside out, tossed onto the closet floor, trashed with the smell of cigarettes and beer, or a silver banana clip missing some of its teeth or a Pink Floyd poster curling at the edges because the tape had come loose, and you wondered how they could be so careless with their beautiful things. Before you left, you placed the sweater in the hamper, you retaped the poster to the wall, and you pocketed the banana clip. You fingered the caps of their shimmering lip glosses. You knew this was risky, but you couldn't help yourself. No one ever caught you.

You would steal the same glittery beads you photographed draped along their vanity mirrors.

When the store manager called and asked your mother to come down to the department store, she almost hung up on him. "Impossible. You must have the wrong girl. My daughter's an honor student, an award winner. Lisa's a tutor, not a thief."

The man assured her that the two girls were one and the same.

After he hung up, the store manager asked you, "Who's Lisa?"

PHOTOGRAPHS DOVETAILED into J. Crew catalogs, trips to the Polo store, and a dorm filled with girls who hailed from Connecticut; Maine; and Great Neck, Manhasset, and Syosset, Long Island. They went to prep schools, they summered on the Vineyard, they owned platinum Rolex watches that cost more than used cars. Freshman year in college and you were in a playground, and everyone was vanilla scented and preened.

You discovered you had a sense of humor and people wanted to be around you because of it. You were the funny girl everyone wanted to dress. You didn't have to sneak into closets anymore; the pretty girls invited you in now, left their doors wide open. You borrowed cashmere, silk, and angora.

You ordered from the catalogs, L.L. Bean and J. Crew, anything you could get your hands on, and you hid the accumulating piles in your closet. The words henley, roll-neck, and gabardine entered your vocabulary; you went from acrylic to double-ply cashmere and lambswool. You made cutouts and wrote "Someday this will be you" on the pictures of preppy models lounging in lakeside cabins. You hoarded books on etiquette, stole flatware from the cafeteria, and practiced setting a table on your bed. From your best friend and roommate, Laurel, you learned the correct way to pronounce *Massachusetts*. Within a year, you sounded as if you were born in New England. Your friends listened to alternative and classic rock and you quickly memorized all the bands' lyrics and hung Pearl Jam, Led Zeppelin, and Nirvana posters on your walls, too.

One night you borrowed your friend Jessica's diamond studs, and at a $5 all-you-can-drink happy hour, you discovered that drinking was a much better way to blend in. When you were drunk, everyone was blurry to you. You were loud, confident, and popular. By your senior year, you had become a Brooks Brothers suit–wearing Merrill Lynch intern who blacked out three nights a week.

You were triumphant over your own creation.

AFTER THE STERN's shoplifting incident, there was a rampage—your mother was a hurricane, moving about the house, throwing books, breaking glasses. But after a few weeks, she forgot the incident, forgot you, and went back to hiding in her bedroom, self-medicating. You were spinning, angry that no one noticed you. You stole money from gym lockers, but that wasn't enough.

The next time you were caught stealing was worse. You were the most trusted student in high school, you had keys to teachers' lounges and offices; as usual the teachers took pity on you because you could never fit in, never had friends to eat lunch with. So you ate your peanut butter and jelly sandwiches in your Spanish teacher's office on Monday, your guidance counselor's office on Tuesday, and your social studies teacher's office on Wednesday. You had become the high-honors darling, second-chair clarinet, and after-school tutor. Then you used your keys to open doors to open purses to open wallets of the women who trusted you most. Over a month you stole three hundred dollars, two credit cards, and a picture of your guidance counselor's daughter.

They caught on to you; they planned a sting operation to catch you in the act. One Friday morning in the spring of your senior year, you managed to break every one of your teachers' hearts.

The principal called your mother at work, called Gus at the farm, and two hours later they surrounded you in an office, trying to pinpoint what exactly was wrong with you.

When you started crying, your mother said, "Save it. Your teachers should be crying for ever trusting you."

Shocked, your principal said, "I'm not sure that's necessary, Mrs. Sullivan. I think there's more going on here than the stealing."

"What's going on, Mrs. McNamara, is that my perfect little daughter has two faces. And it's Ms. Sullivan."

Gus fixed his gaze on his shoes, but when you couldn't stop sobbing, he held out his hand to you. Your mother pushed it away, cut you with her eyes, and said, "I'm so ashamed of you." Hers was the loudest voice in the room.

You told anyone and no one in particular that you were so sorry.

Hands folded, your principal looked you in the eye and said calling the police was the last thing she wanted to do, and she ignored your mother's interruption about how that was exactly what she should do. Your principal made you a deal. This incident would go away quietly if you saw a therapist for six months. She told you that this was not a negotiation.

In the intake session your mother, Gus, and you sat in a room with a blond therapist named Laura, who was possibly in her mid-twenties. Your mother chain-smoked, ignoring the No Smoking signs, and scowled, repeatedly reminding your therapist that she was only here to help her daughter, that she was not the crazy one.

Your therapist said she preferred not to use the word *crazy*.

"Of course you do," your mother said.

When Laura asked you why you stole the clothes and the money, you said you didn't know, and your mother said, "Because she's a fucking thief, why else do you think? Do you know how ashamed I am? Did you ever stop to think how this would humiliate *me*?" She got up, started pacing, knocking things over. You hid your head between your knees and you told yourself to keep breathing, it would be over soon.

Your therapist, visibly shaken, asked your mother to sit down. But there was no stopping her, she went on a fifteen-minute tirade about how worthless you are, how she never beat you, she never locked you in a bathroom for days at a time without food or water. "You have it so good and you fucked it up," she said.

"You see, Laura, this is how it always is," Gus said softly.

"Ms. Sullivan, please sit *down*," Laura said.

Your mother said to you, "I don't even know who you are."

For once, your mother and you were in complete agreement.

When you mother collapsed into her chair, she reminded you of your aunt Marisol.

Laura asked you again why you had taken those things, and you looked up and said, "I'm so angry."

"What are you angry about?" she asked.

You looked at your mother, whose hands began to quiver as she tried to light another cigarette, as if igniting it were the one thing she did care about, and you said, "I'm angry with her."

The Vertical Journey

LONG ISLAND/BRONX

1996–1997

A WEEK BEFORE CHRISTMAS, we celebrate my twenty-first birthday by burning my fake ID. I'm no longer Kiki Hodowatta from Bogota, New Jersey. We throw a lavish house party as only we know how, replete with a full bar and an Italian feast. Bottles of Southern Comfort, Jack, and Absolut line our living room table, and the kitchen teems with hot trays of lasagna and roasted eggplant. The girls have baked me an iced carrot cake, which, for some reason, resembles a peach mountain showered with pink sprinkles. They take a picture of me with a butcher knife, poised to slice, blowing out the candles. The girls bring wine, white Zinfandel, and the boys bring cases of Rolling Rock and Coors Light. We are college seniors. We toast my liberation, my coming of drinking age. We drink until we see black.

I don't remember leaving our apartment, but apparently we do. Days later, people will tell me that they'd never seen me so happy.

SEVEN MONTHS AGO my mother had told me that she'd never been on a plane. Her voice was tinged with envy. She leaned over, ate the food off my plate. Crumpled her napkin into my water glass. Now I was leaving for Chicago for my summer auditing internship with Reuters.

"You go up in the air and come down. Like being on a roller coaster. It's not entirely special," I said, although I knew that to her it was.

"They're paying for your ticket, this company, your hotel, *everything*?" my mother asked. Last year, in a shopping frenzy, she'd purchased half the Mandee juniors' section. She groped accessories, stuffed pearl hair clips and velvet scrunchies in her basket. Tore apart the sales racks with the ferocity of a caged animal. My mother bought skirts two sizes too small because she claimed that she only needed to lose a little. Incentive skirts, she called them. Today she wore white patent-leather sandals with gold buckles and one of the incentive skirts, which was held together by a platoon of safety pins and gold thread, her stomach expanding because of all the six packs she drank to ease the inevitable crash landing from cocaine, while the rest of her body was frighteningly thin. Her eyes were covered in violet glitter.

"Of course they're paying, anything can be expensed," I said.

Nodding, she picked at the bread. "You must be important. They must need you."

"Imagine that," I said. I tried to locate the waiter. My eyes roved the dusty bar shelves, pining for warm, sweet comfort. People had been talking about my mother again. She was convinced she was my age, wearing tight shirts and platform heels to bars. As soon as I left for college, she took a taxi to the local bars and befriended all those people who despised me in high school. She'd been seen shooting pool in cheap dive bars with my former classmates. People heard her laugh at jokes made at my expense; my mother smoothed her fine hair and said that her daughter certainly didn't get her hair from her—"Lisa is who she is because of her father," she said. I heard they were momentarily confused because my name wasn't Lisa. People whispered that she shared her drugs with my enemies, high-school graduates who still lived with their parents, who were content to drive around Valley Stream in circles, going nowhere. They saw her toss back shots of tequila with the boys who had thrown boxes of Brillo at me in calculus, who had knocked books out of my hands and howled as they scattered along the corridor. Now the boys drove their banged-up IROC cars to their auto-body jobs, picking up Hewlett cheerleaders, cruising the mall and Grant Park on the way. People saw her roll spliffs with the spiky-haired girls, the ones who had called me white nigger. Now they shampooed hair in salons, suffered beatings from their white-trash boyfriends.

"They won't serve you here," my mother said, slurping at the last dregs of her piña colada, stirred frothy coconut milk with a curved straw. Why must she slurp? Why must she always chew with her mouth open? pick at her teeth with her nails? I was embarrassed for her; she had no idea how low-class she was. "This isn't the *city*." Before I left for college, I drew an imaginary line between my mother and me. I vowed never to cross over to her side. I would never be like her. We were in an Italian restaurant on Rockaway Avenue.

"Doesn't matter, I'm leaving soon. The four fifty-two," I said, pointing to my watch.

As my mother blathered on about some new waitress who pilfered tips, stiffed the busboys, and stole tables, I ripped open Sweet 'N Low packets. Emptying the contents on the table, I formed mountains while my mother's lips moved.

Over the past three years, our relationship had been reduced to these painful semiannual lunches in local diners where we interrogated each other with the same sterile questions about work and school over oily food—filler conversation with minor variations. Anything to evade the possibility of an uncomfortable silence. We bulldozed our way through appetizers, chicken, pasta, and coffee. And while Gus frequently visited Fordham, my mother never set foot in a car that would take her to my college, because she refused to visit me in a place where she should have gone. Because of me she couldn't finish college. I stole what was owing to her—a college education. So I described it to her in excruciating detail. She had never seen the tall, elegant black gates surrounding the beautiful, lush campus that made me immediately fall in love, the lawns where we played Frisbee and sketched, blasted Pearl Jam and

Nirvana until late in the evening, the small church with its stained glass windows and golden chalice, the Gothic buildings where our philosophy and religion classes were held; my mother removed herself from my new life and the woman I was slowly becoming. My transformation must have unnerved her, because she squirmed whenever I talked about a career in investment banking, flinched on the few occasions on which I met her dressed in a suit. I had surpassed her; I was independent and didn't need her. She knew this and I knew she hated it, right down to my matching leather loafers and handbags.

We passed like night—me rising, her falling. As a child I viewed her as sexy, carnivorous, strutting down Brooklyn streets in her black leather coat—the seventies were kind to her—but now I could see her clearly as withered, discounted, small. Lines crept up around her eyes, above her brow. Years of hard living had marked her face. But she still saw herself as she did then: young, glamorous, and defiant. And she maintained a closetful of nostalgia: polyester suits, green hip-huggers, and chunky shoes, preserved in plastic bags.

While my mother complained about the slow summer season, her meager earnings, I realized that I couldn't care less about the goings on at the sleepy Jackson diner on Sunrise Highway in Valley Stream, the waitresses chain-smoking and gum-smacking, counting their tips. Fighting over stations. Sleeping with the Greek bosses for better shifts. But my mother and I continued to speak at each other, staring sideways. We kept these lunches. Perhaps to test how long we could endure each other.

In the end, when she finished her tirade, we tallied the check, split it two ways. I had a train to catch; she had her crossword puzzles and her couch.

"I have something to tell you," my mother said, as I slapped down my credit card, taking her cash.

"My train," I protested.

"I met someone," she said.

"What are you talking about, you *met* someone? You *have* someone, his name is Gus, remember?" I said, tightly.

GUS APPLAUDED AT my recitals while my mother lay in her bed, knitting, needles clinking. "Leave the awards on the table. I'll look at them later," she said. Always they ended up on the floor. My senior year in high school, Gus cried when the Spanish department awarded me a certificate of excellence. On the way home we stopped at 7-Eleven for smokes and ginger ale. While Gus was inside, my mother and I sat silent with the motor running. She sucked her teeth. I kicked the back of her seat.

"Watch it," she said.

"Watch what?" I said.

Rolling up the windows, she let the car fill up with her cigarette smoke. She was fuming. "You were supposed to win the writing award. Some writer you are. What a waste of my fucking time," she said.

When Gus came back, a bag balanced on his arm, he opened the door and all the smoke rushed out and I was crying and coughing and my mother was puffing. In front of our house, I yelled out to her that I tried so hard.

"I hate you," I said. She turned around, scowling the way she always did.

"You don't have to live here. You're free to go."

She never conceived of my leaving.

"Who is he?" I asked now. "This man?"

"My man's name is Tom. We met in a bar, of all places," my mother said.

"What?" I couldn't believe the words coming out of her mouth. "This is some sort of cruel joke, right? Because it must be."

"He's sexy. Tall, blond hair, and a moustache. He takes me dancing. Lisa, I tell you, before him, I couldn't remember the last time I danced."

"I'm not sure how you expect me to react to all this. What do you want from me?" I asked, livid.

"I don't want nothing," my mother said, lighting a Kent. She wasn't remorseful of her betrayal; in fact, she seemed *relieved*.

"Anything," I said. "If you don't want nothing, you want something."

"Stop with that shit. You couldn't even believe the *sex* . . ."

"I don't want to hear this." But she kept telling me that she wanted a real *man*, a real *life;* and the space between my mother and me had grown so wide, I didn't know how to close it. It had gotten too big for me to wrap my arms around.

"I'm finally *happy*," she said, "and I thought you should know. About my happiness."

"Your happiness is making me sick." I could see joy in her face, the way her hazel eyes glinted as she spoke. I'd hadn't seen that in years — signs of life, of love.

"For once, can this not be about you?" my mother said.

"Because it's never about *you*," I said.

"He's taking me to Disney World." She was gushing now. "Soon I'll be on a plane. Like you."

My mother was leaving my father for mouse ears, cotton candy, and amusement park rides.

"Good for you." I gathered my things. When I stood to leave, my mother grabbed my wrist tight. She was always stronger. "Let go," I said.

"Don't take this away from me," she said, pointing her cigarette at me. "It's not fair, all that you have. Don't be so fucking *selfish*."

"Selfish? I guess that's what you would think."

"I'm leaving Gus. I wanted you to hear it from me," she said. She tapped a nail on the table. Then she paused, her finger midair, midtap. "But we could be friends. We could see each other once in a while. Like this. I can't give you my number; Tom and I need to settle in, get used to living together. But I'll call you. I just don't want to see you for a while."

I felt like one of her torn photographs. She might have scissors under the table, poised, ready, because here she was, sitting across from me, cutting me out of her life.

"Right," I said. Shaking my wrist free, I wondered how I could be friends with someone I wasn't even sure I loved, much less liked.

"Lisa," she said.

"For once can you call me Felicia?"

In Chicago, the Marriott Residence Inn was located across the street from the posh Drake Hotel, and on my way home I caught a glimpse of Princess Diana exiting the gold revolving doors. An eggplant gown draped her tiny body, and she waved to the maelstrom of flashbulbs and fuzzy microphones that sprouted from behind police barricades. Their hands gripping photos of her, fans pleaded for autographs. *"Diana,"* they shouted, *"look here!"* A man held her head as she ducked inside the limo.

Inside my hotel room, the red message light blinked furiously. The first message was from my mother: "I just wanted you to know—" I hung up and dialed home.

"She's gone," Gus said. He was breathless, frantic. I could hear him pacing the rooms, his sneakers squeaking.

"What do you mean, she's gone? Where did she go?"

"I don't know. She hasn't been home in a week. . . ." It wasn't like the old days with Avi, when my mother would disappear for weeks at a time. The past few years she stayed away a night, two at most.

"A week? Wait, rewind. Tell me what happened."

"I didn't want to worry you," he said.

"I'm worried."

"We had this huge argument, God, I don't even remember

how it started. She said all these things, evil things, you wouldn't believe. Well, maybe you would. That I was worthless; I could never give her the life she wanted. And then she left; you know how your mother gets. But I didn't phone you because she always comes back." Gus paused. "Did you know she's been seeing some other man for *two years*? Remember when she went out last Thanksgiving for cigarettes, when she was gone for six hours? She was with *him*."

"Two years?" I felt nauseous.

"So today, out of nowhere, she rode up in a taxi. Kept the motor running. Ran in the house like she knew exactly what she wanted. She went for the TV, some of her clothes, and—oh, for fuck's sake, you wouldn't believe . . . went through *your* photo album and started pulling out pictures of *herself.* The bitch left without saying a word."

"And you didn't stop her? You didn't ask her where she was going? For fucking *Chrissake* . . ." My hands started to shake.

"As if I could stop your mother."

When he hung up, my whole body was numb. I lay my palms on the mattress and pushed down to feel a slight bounce of the bed.

The next morning I boarded a standby flight, and two turbulent hours later I arrived in Newark. Sweaty, I dragged two ripped shopping bags and a massive suitcase the length of the terminal, searching for Summit Car Service. After traipsing through all the arrival areas, I found my driver stomping his foot impatiently, his T-shirt underarms revealing half-moons of perspiration.

On the parkway I called Gus, who proceeded to lecture me on the dangers of cell phone usage and the possibility of brain damage.

"Are you close?" he asked.

"I'm close," I said, through static. "But I'm losing you."

"I'm here," he shouted.

"No, you're cutting in and out. I have to go."

"Tell me, Lisa, where does everyone go when they say they have to go?"

When I arrived home, Gus was waiting for me on the stoop, head in his hands.

I knew then that I'd have to shoulder all of this, her leaving and its consequences.

"We have to move," he said. "We're months behind in rent and Tim and Betty are fed up. They want us out."

"By when?"

"I've never been evicted," he said.

"When, Gus, *when*?" I said. I glanced at his hands—practical, working hands, not equipped to handle complexities.

"Within a month." Shaking his head, he continued, "How will we find a place, get the money? I wouldn't even know where to begin." I knew he wanted to say, "But *you* do."

Dropping my bags, I stood at the head of the lawn, only a patch of concrete dividing us, and I wanted to be tissue. Lift me up; blow me away. High up in the trees where no one can find me.

Gus looked up at me, pleading with those hopeful eyes. I would be the soldier; I would have all the answers. He needed me to bear the weight of his head in my hands. But I grew terrified. I feared that I would become vulnerable in ways that I'd never imagined. I would become a person I couldn't control.

"Let's go inside," I said.

IN WENDY'S ON Merrick Road, we cruised the salad bar, piling cucumber slices and shredded lettuce into our plastic bowls. We promised ourselves we'd be good but it felt necessary to toss the salad into the garbage and be bad. Gus ordered the bacon cheeseburger and large fries; I dipped French fries into a cup of tepid cheese. Two soggy baked potatoes lathered in sour cream and bacon bits remained on my plate, ready to be devoured. Sheryl Crow played over the speakers. Reckless teenagers left their trays teeming with napkins covered in their satiny lipstick. They abandoned their tables, one by one, large cups toppled, chairs askew, a strip of cheddar glued to the floor.

"Rent is due next week."

"Don't worry, I'll take care of it," I said, "I'll take care of everything."

Why couldn't someone, for once, take care of me?

"LOOK AT THIS PLACE, will you just *look*?" Betty clucked her teeth at her husband. "Filth everywhere."

I held an ignored check in my outstretched hand.

The landlord traced the yellow floral kitchen wallpaper, collecting grease on her fingertips. With her hips she pushed aside my mother's mattress to find piles of ground cigarette butts and empty

Budweiser cans, the floor sticky with dried beer, crossword puzzles half-finished, a slice of moldy peach pie. My mother still lingered; I could smell her Chanel No. 5 in my hair, as if I could so easily take on her scent like an article of clothing that could be worn or shed. Betty flared her nostrils as she clipped through the rooms; her rose-tinted glasses perched on the bump of her sweaty nose. Her eyes filled with disgust. I noticed a bald spot on her head.

"What human lives like this?" she asked.

"We'll have to reevaluate the lease," Tim said.

"Aren't you ashamed of this?" Betty gestured around, pointing to the litter box that made the hallway reek of urine. Feces-strewn pawprints streaked the floor. "Of living like animals?"

"What do you expect," Tim said, "from trash?"

"Pigs sleep in their own shit, it's true," Betty said.

Just take the check and go!

"You'll continue to get paid," I said. "You don't have to worry about the rent."

"Oh, we will. Be paid. We'll be paid for stripping the floors, retiling, cleaning the walls, repainting. You will pay for all of it and then some."

"How will we get this smell out?" Tim said, dramatically clamping his hand over his nostrils.

"*Unbelievable,*" Betty said, revealing yellowed horse teeth.

"You have a month," Tim said.

"We don't want your kind here. Everyone knows about your mother, about all the coke she does, all the punks she hangs out with." Betty swiped the check from my hand.

"A month," Tim said, as they made their way to the door.

"And I want this place cleaned. Spotless. I want to see my reflection off the fucking floors," Betty said. "I want to eat off the toilet lid. Do you understand me?"

I nodded.

"I can't hear you," she said.

"I understand," I said.

And then they were gone. From the bags I brought from the store, I unwrapped sponges, poured the bleach and hot water into the bucket. Laid the dustpan and broom on the floor. Ripped bath towels apart with my hands.

"Do you think we'll get the security back?" Gus asked. We'd been on our knees, scrubbing through the night.

How could he be so blind?

A MONTH LATER it was only Tim who arrived, performing a quick inspection of the pale house. The whitewashed walls, the stove that gleamed, my pruned skin and the cuts on my arms and feet—he took the work in with a succession of approving grunts. Not once did he speak to me, and after ten minutes he left.

We were free.

An hour later the phone rang. Her voice.

"I need you to do something for me," she said. As if it were normal to disappear for a month and then call home.

"Where are you?"

"I need you to phone the diner. Call in sick for me," she said.

"Why can't you call?"

"It's not a good time," she said.

"We got evicted," I said. "Do you know what Betty said about you? What everyone's saying about you, about your drug problem?"

"I don't have a drug problem and I don't have time for this, Lisa," she said, exasperated.

"Tell me where you are."

"Can't you just make the call? Can't you do this one thing?"

"I can't help you," I said.

"You have to," she said.

A part of me longed to obey, to be the good daughter who cleans up a house, bears her family's collective shame, but I was so tired.

"Don't call this number again," I said. "Because we don't live here anymore."

In our house, there is no tree. No silver tinsel, garland, or snow-covered angels. There's no room for any of it. Gus and I sit mute in front of the television. Intermittently we take turns getting up to adjust the antenna. We watch *Roseanne* in silence. Through the laugh tracks, we stir food around on our plates. The mozzarella cheese resembles plastic, the meat is bloodied and greasy, and the pasta is limp, overcooked, but we eat anyway because this is what you do on a holiday. You have dinner, you snicker through grace, and you give one another presents you can't afford to buy.

"What did you do for your birthday?" he asks.

"I got drunk," I say.

Gus shakes his head, clears our plates. "I'm going to take you

out," he says, his voice quivering. "For a proper birthday. You deserve at least that."

"Don't worry about it," I say. And I begin to think that there are
a great many things that I don't have but do deserve.

"Have you heard from your mother?"

"What do you think?" I say. My gaze remains transfixed on the
television screen.

"She didn't even call you on your birthday? Your fucking *birthday*?"

"I would have told you if she phoned," I say. It occurs to me that
we live in a dry house. We're miles from liquor.

He throws the dishes in the sink, grips the counter with his
hands. And we're still like this, he in the kitchen trying hard not
to cry, me on the couch, changing channels.

My mother will not break me. No way in hell will I allow it.

The next morning we wipe the sleep from our eyes. We ride over
sheets of black ice, the wheels slick on the quiet roads.

I check the time.

"You could cry, you know," he says, staring through the windshield.

I check the time.

OUTSIDE, THE WIND makes the windows shake. My room
is cold, dark. A drift forms on the windowsill; the snow threatens
to break away, tumbling thirteen floors to the ground. Above the
telephone booth–shape security station, a uniformed guard holds
post with only his radio to keep him company. I consider opening
the window, allowing air in.

Classes start next week and I've returned to the dorm early. Walsh Hall, with its low ceilings, plywood furniture, and gloomy lights, is my home senior year at Fordham. I live in a suite that rooms four, but it's only me here tonight, weaving through this space, touching my roommates' bedspreads and homemade afghans, drinking Diet Coke straight from the can. My friends are with their families, savoring as much of the holidays as they can before the new semester starts. I fix some pasta with minced garlic and olive oil. I eat in the dark. I'm frightened of sleep.

I set the dishes in the sink now and contemplate phoning Laurel in Connecticut. I want to hear a familiar voice, her throaty laugh traveling across the line. And while we talked of our plans to live together after college, a two-bedroom apartment on the Upper West Side close to all the bars we frequent and the Bally's gym on Seventy-third, a seven-foot tree would be illuminating her safe house. I'd press her to talk a little longer in hopes that some of that light might make its way to this dark Bronx student apartment.

I pick up the phone, start pounding the twenty-odd digits to make an outgoing call, when a voice shouts, "Jesus Christ, you're killing my ears."

"How did you get this number?"

"It's amazing how easy it is to break down an operator on the holidays."

"How did you get this number?" I repeat.

"I didn't *say* I got your number. Don't go assuming everything. The operator put me through. And I wonder if this is any way to treat your mother on the holidays."

"It's January. The holidays were last month."

Five months of silence, and the first time my mother contacts me she's high. The grinding teeth, the constant swallowing, the congestion — this is all familiar territory. I lay the phone down on the carpet. I crawl under my roommate's bed.

"We thought you were dead, we didn't hear from you," I say.

"I'm very much alive," she says. "But I'm having some . . . financial problems."

"What do you want from me?" I say. "I have tuition bills to pay; I don't have any money to spare."

"All that money I spent raising you. Money spent on *you*. I think I'm entitled to some payback. And come to think of it, you gave me, what, $800 from your insurance settlement? I didn't complain then when you cashed your fancy $10,000 check. In fact, I didn't say a word when you gave Gus more."

She's a champion of her own self-pity. My settlement was held in a trust until I was eighteen and now, three years later, my mother feels as if she's entitled to more of my money.

I bite my lip hard. "That money was for *me*, from my car accident. Not for *you*." Why wasn't she there when I was ten, crossing the intersection to buy Cheese Doodles from the store on the other side? Instead, she folded clothes and paired socks in the Laundromat. When the car barreled down the street, it hit me, sent me flying. But what I really want to ask is this: Why did you let me go out on my own?

"Who do you think took care of you after the accident? When you couldn't get out of bed, had to piss in a pan? Part of that money should be for *me*."

"I didn't realize I was being billed," I say, gnawing my bottom lip.

"You owe me," she says. "For so much."

"You can't call here again," I warn, ending the conversation.

"Don't you hang up," she threatens. "You don't go until I say you can go."

"Then let me go." Dust moats settle over my face. I keep chewing my lip. I've become silent in the way people do when you have gone too far with them, asked for too much. A part of my mother must sense that, because I hear her cover the phone. We remain still, inhales and exhales pantomiming one another, until I hear the soft click of the phone, a dial tone.

In the bathroom I turn on the faucets, sink and tub, and I close the door. Steam rises above the shower curtain, feigning smoke. But I'm not capable of setting fires. And it is only when I reach up for the switch to turn off the lights that I see my reflection in the mirror: a swollen mouth; my lower lip blooming like a diseased flower because I have been biting down on it so hard. Before I settle down on the cold tiles, I see my face covered in blood.

I HAVEN'T SEEN my mother cry since I was a child and used to watch her sleep. Her body is a small house, seemingly incapable of sheltering tears. But I remember one afternoon clearly, when I'd come home from school early and found her head smashed into the carpet, Eddie darting a butcher knife to her scalp; she wailed then. Through a faceful of tears and blood, she yelled at me to get out, go, to run out and play. Lock the door behind me. Come back later. Never did she ask for help—even when he broke her jaw in two places. It was as if she played a role: the woman whose bones he could break.

TODAY, A MONTH before my college graduation, my mother phones me and she's crying.

"He tried to kill me," she stutters. "His hands, they were on my neck. So hard, tight, I couldn't breathe. And I tried to be good, to behave, like he wanted me to, and then I made that phone call—I was so fucking *stupid,* because he told me not to use the phone and I shouldn't have used the phone because he told me not to use it. We don't have a phone anymore; he ripped it out of the wall, Lisa. I'm calling you from my neighbor's, downstairs. Can you hear me?"

"Tom," I say. The man my mother left us for. Laurel enters, sees my face, and her books tumble to the floor. Is it possible that I could be whiter? I feel my body cave in on itself, dissolve.

I wave Laurel away. "I'm okay," I mouth.

"No, you're not," she says.

"I did everything he wanted me to," my mother continues. "But then he came to the diner and made this scene you wouldn't believe, and George fired me. Said he couldn't have this in the restaurant, this messiness, it's bad for business. And then the fucker disappeared with all my tips. There are only cigarettes here and some eggs. So I tried to call you and that's when he came back and found me. He tried to kill me when I called you."

My mother doesn't deserve to be strangled.

"You don't deserve this," I say.

"Everything used to be so perfect. He wasn't like this when we met," my mother says, "I don't understand. All the trips we took; he bought me these turquoise earrings."

How do I explain that it never is what you want it to be? "I'll call the police if you need me to. I can dial them now."

"I don't know," she says, nervous. "He's calmed down. You don't know how good he could be. Maybe things will get better."

"Wake up, this man tried to *kill* you. It won't get better."

Laurel sits on her bed, watching.

When my mother doesn't say anything, I ask, "Do you have anywhere safe to go?"

After she confirms that her neighbor could hide her in his basement, a semblance of the woman I know returns. She is vengeful. "Maybe jail will teach him a thing or two."

I write her address on the back of a notebook. She lives in New Hyde Park. A part of me wants to laugh. All this time I've spent wondering where she could be, dissecting towns in which she could live, and here it is, so simple, a street, a town, a house number, all delivered over a telephone line.

"I never knew what I had with you and Gus. He was good to me, and I lost him, lost you both. How stupid could I be?"

I know where she's going with this and I'm uneasy. My mother calls me when she's flailing. When she's less than zero. I could be anyone; it wouldn't matter. I'm the last resort.

"Do you think . . . ? I don't know. Do you think Gus'd take me back? Forgive me."

"You don't get it, do you? Look what you've done." I grip the receiver, knuckles white. And suddenly I think back to when I asked about my real father, and I say, "How could *I* forgive someone who leaves?"

"What are you talking about? *What I've done.* What have *I* done to *you*? You have everything and I have nothing. How are you hurting?"

I clamp my hand over my mouth. I could faint and no one would catch me. The fall would be bottomless, never-ending, and my mother will always be there, pushing me further down. But Laurel rushes over, holds me tight from behind. She bites my shoulder. She's seldom affectionate, physically, so her hold shocks me. "I'm here," she says.

"You make it impossible for me to love you," I say.

"I don't believe this," my mother says. "Who put a roof over your head, that macaroni and cheese that you like on the table, those fancy clothes on your back?"

"Being a mother isn't a favor. It's your fucking *obligation*. And *I* put those fancy clothes on my back. I put myself through school. Not you. But let me tell you what *I've* done for *you*. I cleaned up after you, I took care of Gus for you, I paid the rent for you, I suffered Betty and Tim for you, I was a parent to you, I was the perfect everything, *for you*."

I am surprised by how loud I can be.

Laurel doesn't let go, even when I try to wiggle free.

"Felicia," my mother says, in that bored tone that I've grown to hate, using my given name because she's annoyed. "What I did, my leaving, wasn't so bad. You were strong. You handled it. I really don't know why you're making such a big fucking deal. I'm the one without money, without a house, a boyfriend. Tom tried to kill me, *remember?*"

I collapse to the floor. It will always be about her. This is what it feels like to let go: a cord from my neck finally unwound. Breathe. Release.

"Hang up," Laurel says. "Hang up the phone."

"I have to go," I say. "I'll call the cops when I hang up."

"I was thinking," my mother says, "of coming to your graduation. I was wondering what you thought about that. About me seeing my baby graduate."

"That's not a good idea," I say.

"Hang up," Laurel repeats.

"Are you saying you don't want me to go?"

"I'll call the police; I'll do that one thing for you."

"Are you saying you don't want me to go?"

"I don't want you there."

"Fine," she says coolly. "Well, *fuck you,* then." She slams down the phone.

And for the first time since I was a child, I can finally breathe.

The Burning I Can't Remember
MANHATTAN 2002

IF YOU LOOK REALLY hard you can see them on my legs. *Look,* I tell him. Two circles on the right side of my left leg, whiter than my skin, if you can imagine that. One the size of a quarter, the other a dime. And then the fat round disc of a scar on the right side. Taking off his glasses, he leans in close and squints. My boyfriend, Ben, asks me how I got these scars, how they arrived on my body.

"I don't know," I say, and pause. "I think I know. But I can never be sure." Then I tell him about the tub bath.

When I was four, my mother used to bathe me in the kitchen sink. I was still compact enough to fit inside the square space, where she'd lather me up with soap and lukewarm water. I remember squealing when she tickled me under the knees, the sides of my hips. Places only she knew. I always reached for her. She was never as close as I wanted her to be; her body was always at a remove. She alone would determine how close I could get. Even at four I felt this—her pullaways, her retreats. When the bath was over, my mother swathed me in a soft towel and cradled me in her arms. This was the moment I savored, being brought up under her chin, her breath on my hair. I remember needing her.

A year later, I graduated to the bathtub. Because I was a big girl now. Really, I was frail, underweight—a miniature version of my mother, people always said. She would fiddle with the spigots; she had to get the water just right, warm but not hot. She would fill the tub with Mr. Bubble powder from a white package with a smiling pink bubble man, which filled the tub with suds. One evening Eddie burst through the front door, shouted out her name in that voice I had grown to hate. Obedient, my mother ran to him, leaving the door slightly ajar. All I could recall was my mother begging, her wailing "*No,*" over and over. Dishes shattered against the walls. I heard her knees collapsing to the floor, heard her choking. I lost time then. Years later, my mother told me she had accidentally turned the hot water knob too far. The hot drops spat on my legs like sparks. My mother said she found me with my legs black and still. She said I was taken to a hospital, covered in white gauze, drugged. She said when the black faded, all that remained were white scars.

"Conversation pieces," I say, nervously laughing at my boyfriend's puzzled face. I get nervous often.

And my mother had told me that the burns didn't scare her but what really frightened her was my silence, how I accepted the pain. "Normal children scream, they cry," she said, "but you were so quiet, I didn't understand it."

The scalding water, the charred legs, the hospital—I remember none of this.

So I tell Ben that my mother had a way of altering memory. There was no real or fake, only the way my mother told it. I was her story and she my author, as she would often remind me. And this inevitably left me confused, her constantly altering my history to a point where I never knew what was real or what was her invention.

Over twenty years later, I fumble for pieces of artifact that are not tainted by her voice. For things that are real.

The First Daughter
BROOKLYN 1988

"WE HAVE NO FAMILY," my mother told me when I was twelve. She was leaning over the sink, washing morning dishes.

"But what about my grandmother?" I asked. I had met my grandmother once, months ago, at a diner on New Utrecht. She flew in from Nebraska after my aunt Marisol died of heroin overdose. We never attended Marisol's funeral, because there was none; my mother told me that she was gone, dead, boxed up in a coffin and buried in Brooklyn somewhere, end of story. My grandmother made all the arrangements. For the few weeks she visited, she stayed in Marisol's old apartment, sleeping between her dead daughter's sheets, but she didn't appear to mind; it seemed that the only thing my grandmother cared about was hounding my mother for forgiveness. For what, I didn't know.

My mother said quietly, "I did all I could for Marisol, and look what she did to herself. She didn't deserve that kind of death, and now I've got that witch of a mother harassing me on the phone, asking if we could be friends. As if I would ever reconcile with that woman." My grandmother called her constantly until my mother took the phone off the hook. Two days later my grandmother rang our doorbell and shouted into the intercom that she would ring the bell the whole goddamn day if she had to. Finally Avi urged my mother to go see her.

"See what she wants and then be done with her," he said. "You could finally get her out of your life." Downstairs, through the locked door, my mother said that she would see her in two hours, for lunch. "I'll give you a half hour of my time," my mother said. "Not a second more."

Now SHE WAS drying dishes. "I don't have a mother anymore. Forget you ever met her," my mother said.

It was hard *not* to remember her—that hair! When we walked into the diner, my grandmother was sitting alone in a booth, waiting, her clown-red bouffant piled high; her eyes were dark green and glinting. Silver bangles lined her arms. She looked nothing like us, morose and dark haired. Their conversation resembled an interview—my grandmother asked about my mother's life and my mother responded with one-word grunts and scowled. My grandmother kept making jokes to fill the silences. I had band practice in the evening, so I had brought my clarinet along and played songs for her.

They talked about Marisol, how no one could have stopped her from using heroin.

"I loved my little wild child," my grandmother said mournfully.

"Give me a break. Where were you when she was shoving needles in her arms? I'll tell you where you were—fucking some nigger plumber in Nebraska. I was Marisol's mother, *I* took care of her."

As we were getting ready to leave, my grandmother leaned in to hug me, and my mother shielded me with her arm. "Don't even think about it," she said.

"I just want to hug my granddaughter. Is that so wrong?"

My mother pulled me closer to her. "She's mine," she said.

"You'll never forgive me for leaving, will you, Rosie?" My grandmother sighed.

Outside the diner, my mother told me stories, horrible ones, about her mother locking her in a dark bathroom for days without food. She beat my mother with belts and wrenches. She brought home a multitude of men who liked my mother's long, wavy hair and hazel eyes. They wanted to play house with the eldest daughter, and so my mother played with these men, she said, until her mother came home. It seemed as if pregnancy was an annual event in their house, because after she had my mother, my grandmother had given birth to six other children, all from different fathers, all of various races.

"We got every nationality in our family," my mother said snidely.

189

I'd only known two of her siblings: Marisol and Carmen. She adored her brother, Michael, who, she said, died in Vietnam.

In the kitchen, my mother wiped down countertops. "You think my mother was evil? She was a fucking princess compared to my grandmother. Remember what I told you about my grandmother? She called me the black devil, kicked me in the stomach when I was carrying you. That rotten bitch had the nerve to tell me that it was for my own good. She was making sure that I couldn't bring another devil into the world." My mother paused, smiling. "I waited for that bitch to die just so I could spit on her grave, and I did." There was pride in her voice.

"They should've never been mothers," she continued. "Look at what they did to me. You're lucky. I never beat you, never locked you in a bathroom. I'm so good to you."

I was expected to hate my mother's family just as much as she did, but I didn't even know her mother. She seemed nice, funny—just as I had imagined a grandmother would be. I wondered what was so wrong about wanting to be part of a family. Why was it always my mother and me against the world?

When my mother left the room to get ready for work, I realized that I couldn't remember my grandmother's name.

"OUR MOTHER NEVER laid a hand on us," my Aunt Carmen said. She was making my favorite, scrambled eggs and ketchup. I was spending the weekend with my aunt and her boyfriend, Romeo, in their apartment on Fourth Avenue. Avi and my mother had just gotten in the station wagon and driven off.

"I don't understand," I said. "My mother told me . . ."

"All I'm saying is that if Rosie said she was getting beat up, we never saw it. We all know Rosie and our mother didn't get along, we just didn't know why."

"Is she still living with that *Jew?*" Romeo asked, walking into the kitchen, wearing only denim shorts and a bandana around his head. His greasy hair fell past his shoulders. He wore a necklace made of feathers. I liked Romeo. We played crazy eights and gin rummy, and he told me stories from when he was in the navy, about all the places he'd seen. Romeo was the only man who treated me like a child instead of a love interest. He made me feel safe.

I said yes, but that I didn't like Avi very much. After I said this I concentrated on my shoes. Lately, the way Avi wanted me to call him "daddy" made my skin crawl. He started giving me that look, the same look Eddie used to give me when my mother was at work and Eddie said he couldn't sleep without a pretty girl in his bed.

"Romeo, please," Carmen said. "Don't start in on Rosie again. It's her life, she can do what she wants."

Romeo must have sensed something wrong, because he said, "If he goes near you, let me know. I'll take care of him."

"*Romeo,*" Carmen pleaded.

Before I left that weekend, my aunt said, "I wouldn't believe everything your mother says. Sometimes Rosie has a way of telling stories: Some of it's real, but a lot of it is in her head."

I nodded, wondering who was telling the truth, what was real.

"That's our secret, okay?" she said, nervous when my mother walked through her front door.

MY MOTHER STARED into the car mirror, fixing her face. She applied frosted lipstick. "How's my little sister?" she asked. "Does she still jump when her big, bad boyfriend snaps his fingers?"

"Spic trash," Avi muttered as he drove.

"You wouldn't say that to his face," I snapped.

"You think I'm scared of the big man? I'm not scared of him," Avi said, but I knew he was. Whenever my mother visited Carmen, Avi stayed in the car, kept his head down low should Romeo ever come out of the house.

"Listen to me," my mother said, suddenly angry. "The woman in that house is weak. I'm embarrassed to call her my sister. You like her boyfriend so much? You wouldn't like him after you saw the bruises on her body and you wouldn't like all the women Romeo brings home to their bed. Four years she's been with that man and he'll never change. Give it another year and I promise you my whore mother will be back to pay for another funeral."

I never saw any bruises. Romeo and Carmen never fought; in fact, they seemed so perfect, planning their family, saving what they could for a little house they wanted on Long Island. When I was with them, they treated me like their daughter. We were a pretend family, albeit for a short while. We played cards, we cooked dinners, we watched game shows.

I didn't believe her.

I looked at my mother looking at herself in the mirror, and I wanted to leap into the front seat and say "What about you and

Eddie? You spent three years with him, how are you different?" It was as if she sensed what I was thinking when she said, "I left Eddie. I was stronger."

"I love them," I blurted out.

"You love *me*," my mother said.

IN FEBRUARY, AFTER SCHOOL, my friend Elena and I walked past Carmen and Romeo's apartment. It had been months since I'd seen them. The curtains in the front window had changed to blinds. There was a toy fire engine on the sill. Elena and I rang the bell, and a fat woman in a floral dress said, *"Los movieron. No residen aquí más."*

They moved?

I ran all the way home.

"Did you know that they moved?" I asked my mother, breathless.

"Who moved?"

"Carmen and Romeo."

"Of course I knew. They bought a house in Forest Hills two months ago."

"Why didn't you tell me?" I shouted.

"Don't raise your voice at me," my mother warned. She sat upright on the couch, tipping ashes into an empty beer can. "I think it's better you don't see them anymore, Lisa. With Carmen not being able to have a child, and you always hanging around . . . it confuses them. They need to start fresh, on their own."

"Hanging around? You dumped me on them!"

"They're not your parents," she said, "and besides, I lost their new number."

"I don't believe you," I said. "*You* don't want me to see them."

My mother laughed. "You have no choice but to believe me."

Reunion

ON THE PHONE we have easy conversation. College best friends, Laurel and I haven't spoken in four years. Tucked away in a trunk are the photographs of us in cap and gown, our faces in profile. We cover the safe topics: jobs, significant others, degrees acquired, and former college friends who, for some reason or another, don't speak to us anymore. Five years ago our roommates and closest friends, Heather and Ciara, both returned the invitation to Laurel's wedding with only the words "respectfully decline." In March I ran into Heather in a bar and after twenty minutes of her artful dodging, I confronted her. She warily eyed my glass of wine, as if this was like old times, when one glass would magically transmute into two bottles and she would have to carry me home from a bar. She and her Dewar's couldn't get away fast enough.

"Whatever," Laurel and I say in unison. We agree that our former roommates are obviously deranged. We're good at that, I think, displacing blame. I mute the television. I can't bear canned laughter.

Laurel is a mother now. And an accountant. She has the life I used to want: neat, uncomplicated, and comfortable. I used to envy her easy life—an affluent, addiction-free family, the house in Connecticut, her fine blond hair and how she used it to get exactly what she wanted—but now, as she raves over *Consumer Reports* magazine and laments over trading in her two-seater Mercedes for a sensible family car, I'm grateful that we are two very different women.

"What giving birth is like," she says, "you couldn't imagine. I can't put it into words. But you're the writer; you'll probably describe it better. Show everyone just how amazing it is."

She proceeds to detail her twenty-hour labor, and we laugh when she confesses to screaming for the Demerol shot, because drugs never belonged to Laurel, they were exclusively mine. Throughout the phone call she never says the words cocaine or addiction, never addresses our breakup directly; she simply refers to the four years we haven't spoken as the "disagreement" or "that thing that happened." Bluntly I remind her that I was a human train wreck, a mess, a woman who needed a bottle of wine and half a gram to get through her day.

"Look how far you've come," she says, hopeful.

"I've got a way to go, still," I say. I tell her that I've cleaned house, rid myself of friends connected to my old life, the ones who party to the light hours. Proclaiming themselves rock stars, they leave incoherent messages on my voice mail, they beg me: Just one drink. Come out for one, like we used to. But I know me, one drink becomes seven, and the following morning I'd wake trying to piece together how I managed to humiliate myself this time.

I tell her I live a safe life. That's the only way.

"That must be good for you," she says. "No temptations."

And although I haven't touched cocaine in three years and I never allow myself more than two glasses of wine a week, I now bemoan my age: *I'm too old for this,* I'm a woman who turns down shots, a woman who leaves a bar with people still in it, maybe on their third round, to ride the subway home, to take comfort in the ten o'clock news, to know that every night it will be on at precisely ten. I need routine, and I confide to Laurel that I'm still shaky, that if tempted, if I've been drinking, I don't know whether I could say no, if it would be that easy to *respectfully decline.* Addictions don't disappear; they lie dormant.

There is an uncomfortable silence. You can practically taste the distance between her home in Connecticut, and mine in Brooklyn.

"Tell me about your son," I say.

And we go on for an hour like this, regaling details about our lives, exchanging anecdotes and the stories that once made us laugh out loud.

"Did you have to go to rehab for . . . ?" I can tell the question causes her discomfort. The fact that she wants to know, but only the broad strokes, not all the details, softens me.

"My coke problem? The binge drinking?" I say, "No, at first I did group work at this place called Smithers, then I went into therapy. I'm a lifer," I tease.

I think about Laurel and me mixing midday cocktails, throwing food in the cafeteria because we could barely see straight. Ten bars in one night didn't phase us. First in the bar for happy hour, still sipping at last call, we were prize-fighting drinkers. We used to kick them back, knock them down, lap them up—we caroused, we were tavern marauders. Back then, Laurel could drink me under the table, under a *house,* and I wondered what made her stop and me go on. Had I been sleeping, had she woken up?

"It's like I'm a diabetic and I have to consistently keep my sugar in check. I guess I'm doing what works for me."

"I want to see you. I miss you." She's timid, unlike herself.

"Sure," I say. "We can do that, meet up." I think I can handle this. A friendship in a new way. I tell myself that I am ready: *You are ready.* We make lunch plans for when I'm tucked away in Easton, Connecticut, working on this book. When I accidentally mistake dinner for lunch on my calendar, out loud, she quickly reminds me that we are meeting for *lunch.* A meal during the light hours, a sandwich, possibly a hamburger. Definitely not cocktails—I know she doesn't mean what I think she means, but does she want to play it safe? Our last dinner in New York, my territory, hadn't gone so well.

"I always thought I couldn't really hurt you. I don't know why I even thought that. Of course I could. Hurt you."

"Forget about it. It's past," Laurel says, in a way that tells me that this is a place she doesn't want to go.

"Did I hurt you?" I ask.

"You scared me," she says.

When she hangs up, my heart pauses. Laurel could be my first friend from the old days to forgive me, and more important, I have finally let my model for the perfect life, her, go.

BEYOND THE WINDOWS tinted blue by the evening and under the actinic sky, the gardens in Easton, the pristine estate in which my kind friend lives, are lush and verdant. Stones pave the winding driveway, and the built-in pool reminds me of an expansive bath, temperate and tranquil; a body of water meant to relieve. Crickets sing in the evening. From my window I can see a lemon tree. My friend has loaned me her cottage, a place where she summers, and upon entering, I drop my bags to the floor, mesmerized. I've never lived in a home that has stairs, a means of separating floors and rooms; we were always boxed in, with only thin walls keeping me from my mother. I spend the good part of that first Monday running up and down the stairs, feeling the carpet tickle my feet.

Tonight I move from room to room taking in the still-life canvases: paintings of half-peeled bananas, champagne grapes, ripened peaches, teapots and kettles done in languid, long brushstrokes.

The attic smells of cedar and wood chips, the basement is musty and dank, as basements tend to be, but what moves me most, where I will spend a great number of evenings, is the family room. The sunken leather chair that takes the shape of my body; the wood-paneled walls; the ceramic-monkey lamps and the stationery desk filled with papers and clothing catalogues, addresses scribbled on scrap paper; framed photographs of gurgling babies held up to the sky, summers at Nantucket and the Vineyard, old-world charm, replete with honey tans and floppy straw hats — all of it reveals a family that doesn't know sorrow. They share facial features: the angled nose, the pronounced jaw, the etched cheekbones and light hair. They know their lineage; they could chart it back a few hundred years if you asked them to. Saxony, Edinburgh, Yorkshire, I'm sure their ancestors built hearths and pyres beyond oceans. They do the things I suspect families do. I used to want that picture life. Yet, I remember that this is a guest cottage and I don't really know whether any of that is exactly true. This family might have concealed its pain well. And the photographs — I'm learning that they can be their own fictions.

As I prepare myself for bed, I think of Laurel. I open all the windows, and outside, starlings weave among trees. I'm curious about whether Laurel lives in a home that has a family room, now that she has a husband and a child.

Restless, I make fists and remind myself that I can do this. I can survive this lunch without choking on the history. And it's okay that my perfectly ironed straight hair has curled up into tight ringlets from too many laps in the pool, and it's fine that the last time Laurel saw me I was doing lines on my dresser amid her tears, her telling me that she will take me home to Connecticut with her, that she will do everything it takes to make me better, and me barking back that I'm not hers to save. "God," I yelled at my trembling best friend, "like Connecticut is the fucking answer. You're so fucking blind." She kept shaking her head. "I know you," I said. "You laughed at my Christmas wreath sophomore year. You called it tacky, and didn't I know better?" "Wreath?" she said. "What wreath?" I was devastated when I tossed the snubbed wreath in the trash. In college I lived for her approval; she was my model, a J. Crew, wealthy, Republican ideal. Her opinion of me was paramount: I wore the navy blue suits she recommended, watched the movies she watched, drank the drinks she mixed when she tended bar. So that night four years ago, a part of me secretly enjoyed rebelling against her. I wanted to frighten her; I wanted to see how many lines I could do in front of her. I told her to leave, to find her way out. Forget she ever knew me.

I tell myself that I can weather this.

WERE HER EYES always that blue? I seem to remember them green. Laurel and I are about to hug each other, but we don't know which way to go. After a few awkward attempts, I lean to the left and she pulls me into her. We compliment each other; we look good, healthy. Laurel laments her baby fat, that she has exactly seven more pounds to lose. We lapse into our old roles, her complaining about her body and me assuring her that she's fine the way she is.

"You gave birth less than a year ago," I say. "You look fucking incredible."

"As opposed to just incredible."

"Not everyone can be a size four," I say.

"But *you* look good," she says, scanning my lean limbs.

We get into the car.

We drive to Monroe, a sleepy nearby town with only a handful of shops, a strip mall, and miles of foliage. In the car I fiddle with Laurel's radio dials and somehow we get onto the topic of politics and I make a snide remark about how not even Republicans in New York were stupid enough to vote for George Bush.

She grips the wheel. "I voted for Bush," she says.

"You can't be serious," I say. "How could you be a woman and vote for that man? If it were up to him, a woman would need her husband's permission to go to the bathroom."

"How could *you* not?" We quickly glance at each other. "What's happened to you?" she says.

"I finally learned how to think for myself," I say.

After driving up and down the road, we settle on one of the diners, done seventies style. It's shabby inside, with brown-and-pea-green leather booths, frosted coconut cakes and lemon meringues with cherries dolloped on top revolving in a glass display case. The waitress arrives. This woman with wiry hair and a gentle countenance wipes down our table and chants the soup specials. I'm sitting across from my former best friend, secretly my longtime nemesis, the girl whose life I've always coveted, and I can't decide what to order.

"The pea soup," the waitress says. Pointing to my silk embroidered bag, the waitress compliments my handbag, says it's the most beautiful thing she's ever seen. Laurel grips her Louis Vuitton.

It felt good to be favored for once; that Laurel wasn't the only person everyone fawned over. It felt good to be seen.

"You're not a carbon copy. Everyone's a copy these days. But you're not." She leaves, tends to another table in her section.

I finger my bag's loose threads. It *is* beautiful. A smile creeps.

"*Okay,* then," Laurel says.

Laurel and I discuss her siblings and the fact that her handsome brother, who recently graduated from law school, is legal enough for me to date.

"Law school?" I say, shocked. "I remember when he was in *high* school."

"Don't remind me. We're so old," Laurel says. "What about that man you were going to marry, Ben?"

"Ben is engaged to someone else," I said. "Six months after we broke up, he went and bought a ring for some WASPy scotch-drinking accountant from Greenwich." He fell in love with the opposite of me. Only a few years ago, I was still trying to play that role, be that woman. I had studied Laurel in college for years and all I needed then was a hip flask, a croquet set, and a collection of cashmere polo sweaters. I could blend in again, but it became exhausting to be someone other than who I really was.

"*I'm* an accountant," Laurel says, a little miffed. "From Connecticut."

"It's different, you drink white wine," I joke.

"What makes you think you're better?" she asks.

"Not better," I say, "different."

We glance at each other, acknowledge our eleven years.

Over our platters, I tell her about all the Fordham graduates I've seen on the subways, in restaurants, and in bars. All these random encounters; I conclude that New York is such a claustrophobic city. "Remember Nancy Watson? I saw her a few years ago," I say. Nancy Watson was a transfer student who lived with us junior year. She had long legs, a loud mouth, and a recurring brain tumor. Her body was a house of radiation.

"She died," Laurel says, somber. "You knew that, right? Two years ago. It was in the alumni newsletter."

"You're kidding me. From the tumor?"

"I couldn't believe it," Laurel says. "On the Internet, I found her obituary in the local paper. And would you believe her father died two years before her?"

"She was so *young*," I say. I remember her in her room junior year, hysterical: The cancer had resurfaced. "It eats at you," she cried, "it kills everything. How could something so small kill everything? I don't understand." I held her head, stroked her hair, as she sobbed.

Six years from that morning in our dorm suite, I was dedicated to destroying my body while she was desperate to save hers.

We divide the check and make tentative future plans; we promise to consult our calendars, trade e-mails suggesting dates. The fall will usher in a visit to Laurel's home, a weekend with her new family.

"I'll try not to kill your son when I pick him up," I say, strapping on my seatbelt. "I'm not good with kids. They're sharp, they have a way of figuring me out."

"I was just about to warn you about *him*," she says. "Brady's incredibly active."

"I can't do the baby talk," I warn. "I have to treat him like he's an adult. There's no other way."

"So don't do the baby talk," she says.

We're quiet on the car ride back.

"I'm sorry to lay Nancy's death on you like that," Laurel says, steering with both hands. She used to be fearless, the one-handed driver. Laurel's driving used to give me vertigo—I once gnawed at the seat belt, screamed for dear life on I-95—but now she drives within the speed limit.

I think of quilted caskets, embalming fluid, powder for her face. I've seen dead bodies before—overdosed addicts under basement stairs, another junkie shot in the park, Eddie's mother of a heart attack—but nothing like this; not a twenty-five year old whose life had been stolen from her.

How did I not overdose, not snort one line too many? I was careless, reckless, while Nancy must have taken inventory of all the things she would never see. In the end, I wonder, had she been frightened or did she let herself go peacefully, that final breath easing its way out?

In Easton, Laurel and I sit in the stalled car, and simultaneously we exclaim that we are happy, *so* happy, we did this. But this is not entirely true because we're changed women. We've become adults and we know this. For the first time in eleven years, it feels right to be independent of her.

As Laurel pulls out of the driveway, I remember us, how one day ten years ago we came out of our rooms wearing the same exact outfit, our plain flannels under our J. Crew roll-necks, our denim jeans and brown suede loafers. Pointing to each other, we said that we had to take a picture. We just had to. So we set the camera to automatic, and as the flash went off, we collapsed onto the bed, laughing, holding each other tight, our feet elevated, suspended midair.

Part Three

Where Bodies Go

BROOKLYN 1987–1988

ON THE FIRST day of junior high school we were below street level, in a makeshift courtyard; teachers' aides yelled into megaphones. They herded us into single-file lines, bellowing out assigned "tracks": 7A, accelerated; 7B, basic; 7C, arts; and 7D, accelerated arts. Confused, we pored over our printouts that detailed our tracks and class schedules. Between two buildings, the main and the annex, we would have eight separate classes, eight teachers and a homeroom. The yard was full of the cackling, shouting kids who had gone to the same elementary school, catching up on their summers, reuniting with their crews, plus the cluster of us outsiders, wide-eyed and lost, praying that we could at least find a bathroom. We hoped there wasn't another building for that. It was still morning, but down there it was night, with only narrow bars of sunlight filtering through the iron gates.

Over the summer I had lost twenty pounds, and on this crucial morning I had spent three hours obsessing over my outfit. I tossed aside the tracksuits, leggings, and frayed dungarees. In front of my mother's closet, I leaned in, took a whiff, and sealed the door shut. Everything smelled of her perfume. Nothing fit.

Finally I settled on an outfit my friend Violet had given me, a gray acid-washed skirt set. On the subway I thought of Violet, now living with relatives in New Mexico. No one in the neighborhood uttered her name, and finally, over the past few weeks, the talk—the rumors traded over the steps in hushed tones, the *I knew its*, *I told you sos*—had faded. The memory of her had thinned—as if she had never existed. Come next week, they'd have new stories because there was always a new story. Ruth closed up shop and moved to Bedford Stuyvesant. The loyal customers followed her like disciples; the others found cheaper dealers on Ninth Avenue or in the boarded-up houses behind the C-Town supermarket off New Utrecht. You didn't have to look far to get a fix.

No one ever questioned Ruth's decision to send Violet away, because there you didn't get involved; you minded your own business. You had your own family drama to deal with. You kept it to yourself.

Even though she was gone, I walked up and down her block. I ignored the stares, the eyes, the whispers on the street like bees buzzing. I heard Violet's voice everywhere, from the pavement cracks to the cars cruising down the street. I glimpsed her taffy-colored hair. If I remained here, on this small space of sidewalk, she couldn't leave. She wouldn't have to. I walked in circles in front of her house, until Tia, a fixture on the stoop, called out. "*Mira*, you lost? Go home, *chica*. Don't end up crazy in New Mexico like your friend."

ONCE A MONTH during gym class, aides distributed a plastic bag filled with sanitary napkins, tampons, and outdated pamphlets that promised to prepare prepubescent girls for womanhood. We thumbed through the colored pamphlets, hungry for a morsel of sex. We needed information—what it was, all the ways in which one could do it, and did it really hurt the first time? We would accept scientific diagrams. Anything that showed anatomy. Even the more experienced girls, who'd had their breasts fondled, felt unskilled fingers grope under their skirts, didn't understand how all that panting and sweating produced another one of us.

In junior high school, pregnant women fascinated us with their full breasts, some with purple nipples showing through white shirts, and swelling bellies lugging around miniature versions of themselves. We revered them, pressed our ears to the mothers' tender skin, just to hear a movement, a kick, a bubbling inside. We sought access to the privileged information these chosen women hoarded.

I knew of only one mother my age, Anna, who had run around fifth-grade math class flashing condoms, showing off how wild she was. When Anna got knocked up, her mother pulled her out of school. All the boys had adored Anna for her dimples, Hungarian accent, and dark green eyes, but when she returned in the sixth grade, she appeared depressed, older than her thirteen years. The boys who once fawned over her suddenly feared her; they kept their distance. They found new crushes, less risky girls who wouldn't force them to play house. Already their own mothers lassoed a tight noose around their sons' necks: Who are you talking to, where are you going, when will you be home? The boys didn't want to be delivered from one house of obligation to another, passed around like an offering. Be a good son. Be a good father.

Women ruled like wardens.

This month's pamphlet focused on the menstrual cycle. We huddled around the balance beam with our white plastic bags.

"This is bullshit," Fatima said. "Tell me something I don't know."

"There go the princess," Ivy whistled.

"Who?" I asked.

The girls nudged and nodded in the direction of a tall, ruby-haired girl heading toward the uneven bars. She was dressed in denim overalls and a sleeveless white hoodie, not the mandatory shorts-and-T-shirt gym attire. Chalking up her hands, she swung between the bars with ease, paid no attention to the gym teacher reprimanding her from the other side of the gymnasium. We watched as Ms. Mateo strutted over, huffy, pointing at her outfit with disdain. Midway through Ms. Mateo's lecture, the girl flipped her hair and coolly walked toward the locker room. "Elena, you get back here!" shouted Ms. Mateo.

"Elena Oyola," Fatima said, awestruck.

Elena disappeared through the metal double doors.

"Her name ain't even Elena. It's Vida, but I guess with a name like that, I'd be bitter and want to change it too," Ivy said.

"Her mom's name is *Bertha*," Fatima said. "And you guys, I'm not even bugging when I tell you that I heard Elena did *it*."

"No shit? *Crazy*." Ivy sighed, lacing her sneakers. "Where did you hear that from?"

"Marcus told me."

"Marcus is all talk," I said.

"I heard her sister tried to kill herself," Ivy said.

"No, her sister likes *girls*," Fatima said.

"I hear her family is crazy fucked up. I mean, like, *mental*," Ivy said.

"Why do you call her the princess?" I asked.

"She too cool to hang out with our year," Ivy said, as she unwrapped a piece of watermelon Bubble Yum and offered the pack around. "Rolls with all the ninth graders in the annex."

"What's with her hair?" Fatima said.

"White girls do that. Go messing with their easy hair. Someone should go in there and be, like, HELLO, you're Puerto Rican. Dyeing your hair ain't going to change your last name no matter how light your shade. Elena thinks she's all that because she can pass." Ivy paused. "No offense, Flea."

"Stop calling me that," I snapped. Lisa, Flea—I wished someone would for once call me by my fucking name. "My name's Felicia."

"Chill," Ivy said. "You don't need to get all defensive."

"Wait, why would Felicia be offended about passing?" Fatima asked.

"Because she's white, fool," Ivy said.

"You are?" Fatima turned to me, shocked. "White?"

"No, she's purple. Dumbass," Ivy said.

"Yes," I said. "I am. White."

MY MOTHER SAT in the dark, flicking a lighter. All the lights in our house were extinguished except for that single flash of fire shaped like a teardrop, which rendered my mother ghostly, a chiaroscuro figure with her ebony hair, her face drained of all color.

"What are you doing?" I asked.

"Passing time," she said. "How was school?"

"The same as yesterday."

"You're never home anymore. Look how big you've grown."

"I'm the same height as last year," I said.

"Avi's gone off again to where I don't know . . ." Her voice trailed off.

"He'll come home. He always does."

"We're going to Atlantic City for the holidays," she said.

"Again?" I had begun to dread the all too frequent trips to the casino and the hotel room in which I would be locked up all day.

"I've never left Brooklyn," she said. "This is the only home I know. I was born here, I went to school here, I brought you up here—sometimes, oh God, I wish I hadn't, I wish I knew what I know now—yet it doesn't feel like a home. But I don't know anywhere else. What do you think, Lisa? Is this, this Brooklyn, home to you?"

"What are you taking about?" I crept down to her shins, traced her calf with my finger, my book bag at my side. She pulled away.

Flick. Flick. Flick. The lighter was hissing.

"I'm so tired," she said. "I sleep all day, but still, I'm so tired."

I measured my words carefully. "Maybe you should look for another job."

My mother's chest heaved. "There is no more work for me. People have been talking. All the bosses know each other. Brooklyn is smaller than you think."

"What about Manhattan? You could get another deli job."

"I was lucky to get that one. And I fucked it all up. I should've been more careful."

Flick. Flick. Flick. The lighter would burst. Fluid would explode in her hand.

"Are you okay?" I asked.

"Aren't we always okay?" Her smile was strained. "Didn't we make ourselves that way?"

I reached over and tried to pry the lighter from her hand, but it burned to the touch and I flew back, blew on my palm.

"Careful," my mother said. "You'll burn yourself."

It began with hair. Elena told me that I had wild hair, her sister's kind, and could she comb it? "My sister, Amanda" — who wasn't really her full sister but her half-sister from her mother's first marriage to a black guy, " — is just like you," Elena said. Elena was Puerto Rican, with straight, shiny, naturally brown hair from root to tip. "The white skin but the kinky hair. Although she's mixed and you're not, so I guess that's different. Are you," Elena asked, "mixed?"

"No," I said, "I don't think so. My mother tells me my father's Italian, but I've never met him. She's Irish. Mostly I look like her." As Elena ran a wide-toothed comb through my hair, it felt soothing; I could sit like this for hours.

Elena whispered in my ear, "My sister never lets me touch her hair."

Elena and I became inseparable. Days passed and we split cans of soda, slices of pizza, smokes. She taught me to inhale. We holed up in her bedroom, hanging out and trading clothes. But it was more like me borrowing everything Elena owned. On her knees, she showed me how to correctly roll up my pants. "Like this," she said, tugging at the inseam. Tubes of lipstick cluttered her bed, and she'd spend half the evening darting between my face and a makeup book she owned. Holding up the pictures of various fashion models with feathered hair and lined eyes, my new best friend tried to decide whether I was "winter" or "spring."

Elena lived in the only duplex in a run-down apartment building. Her mother spent her money to distinguish herself from the poor families living in the overcrowded one- and two-bedroom apartments. Awed, I ran up her carpeted stairs and back down again. No one in my neighborhood had an apartment that occupied two floors. We lived in buildings with shattered windows, smashed-in mailboxes, bells that never worked. Yet here was a fish tank that spanned an entire wall in the living room. When we moved in with Eddie, he bought my mother a gigantic tank, filled

it with coral, turquoise rock, and seaweed. The fish were silver, orange, and blue, with swaying fins. Eddie bought her a small shark
and named it Killer. As I stood over Elena's tank, shaking food
flakes into the water, I remembered how Eddie starved every last
one of my mother's fish.

Elena warned me that the closets as well as her sister's room
were off-limits. I asked her how she had all this, the carpeting, the
sound system, the fish. Chewing ice, she said her mother was a
nurse and her father's life insurance policy paid for the apartment
they owned. I was learning that Elena's father was off-limits, too.

We fixed tuna sandwiches with ground-up potato chips and
mayonnaise. Elena lavished attention on me, specifically on trans-
forming me, and at first I didn't mind.

"YOU NEED TO cut class," Elena said, matter-of-factly.
It was late January and unseasonably warm. We passed a smoke
between our fingers, inhaling till the filter smoldered. Elena sug-
gested we get a roach clip. "Break this perfect image you got going
on. I mean, seriously, how do you get such high marks? I'm with
you all the time. Do you sleep?"

And how could I know then that almost twenty years later,
people would pose the same questions. How do you do all the
things you do? Do you sleep? Questions I never felt comfortable
answering. Look at me, but not too close.

"Not going to happen," I said. Cutting class was unfathomable.
I had my limits.

"Missing *one* class won't kill you." But I wasn't fooled. I knew once I gave her one class, she'd take the entire day. Elena acted as though life was to be lived exactly as she wished it. But then her eyes drifted, her lips moved quickly, REM sleep of the mouth. She was gone again. I had grown used to this, her being here but not here.

"We used to cut school. We pretended we were secret agents; we thought no one would recognize us if we dyed our hair. She made me blond. She made herself red. I couldn't touch her hair. We hid under the bed so that no one would find us. Smoked cigarettes and drank rum until we passed out."

"Who's *she*?"

"Amanda."

"What happened? Between you and Amanda."

"We could stay here all day. We'd never have to leave," she begged.

"Let me think about it."

Amanda's room was always locked: a room and a girl I would never see for the entire time Elena and I stayed friends. "She's fucking crazy" is all Elena would say about her sister, who would talk to their mother over the second phone line in her room. Was she a changeling, something gruesome and disfigured, deserving of imprisonment? Was she real? I knew Amanda existed because she often yelled at us from behind her door. Sometimes she thrashed about, throwing things against the wall; other times she sang sad songs off-key. Melancholy drifted into the hallway. "Ignore her," Elena would tell me.

Today her sister was strumming her guitar; she wasn't very good at it.

"You're shouting!" Amanda said. "I can't concentrate with all the noise."

"No we're not," Elena yelled back.

"Then why can I hear you?"

"Maybe we should go," I offered, but I really wanted to stay. Perhaps if Elena pushed her hard enough, got her sister angry enough, I'd catch a glimpse. I'd see the skin, the hair.

"Fuck off," Elena said. Bolting up, she lurched toward the door and struck it repeatedly with the heel of her boot. "We can talk as loud as we want to."

"You and your little follower are pathetic."

"Take your pills, Amanda. Time to take your pills," Elena taunted.

Downstairs, the second line rang, and I could hear Amanda whimpering in the adjacent room.

Elena and I sat down at the top of the stairs. "Vida, I'm warning you," her mother called from the foot of the stairs, the phone in her hand. "Your sister's on the phone and you're upsetting her. We talked about this, Vida. I don't know how many times. How many times?"

"Are you kidding me?" Elena shot back. "I've been in my room since I got home from school. With my *friend*—the smart one I told you about. How could I be bothering *her*?"

"Don't upset your sister. You hear me?"

"I hear you," Elena said, slamming her door shut. Under her breath, Elena said, "One day I'm going to kick that door down, you just wait and see."

"So wassup," Ivy said, cornering me. "You don't walk home with us; you dissed 'Tima in homeroom. What? Now you too cool to kick it with us?"

"I've been busy," I said, avoiding her eyes. Instead I focused on her ponytails, which jutted out like two pompons, and then quickly switched to her sneakers and the floor surrounding them.

"Bull*shit*," Ivy spat. "Flat-leaver."

"I didn't *diss* anyone. I was just finishing my homework before first period."

"Uh-huh, right. Whatever. You gonna eat lunch with us today, or what?"

"I can't," I stammered. "Me and Elena . . ."

"You can't even look me in the eye, Flea," Ivy said. When I didn't respond, she continued, "So it's like that now? It's like that."

"I'm sorry," I said. Tears spilled down Ivy's cheeks. I'd never made anyone cry before. But here she was, hands covering a wet face. "God, I am such a *shit*. I am so sorry, Ivy."

"She ain't going to make you any whiter, Flea," Ivy replied coldly, fleeing down the corridor.

"Look at us, we're air. We've disappeared," Elena said. Under her bed, a white sheet pulled down over her mattress curtained our faces.

We'd been here for an hour. I fidgeted. About now, Ivy and I would be pinching corn chips from the deli on Sixth Avenue. Fatima would prove, once again, that even fat people could do a cartwheel. Within seconds, her feet would momentarily touch the sky, her hands planted on the ground. I left all of that and English class to squeeze my way under Elena's bed and wave flashlights in our faces.

"I'm getting tired," I said.

Elena glared. "Don't you know you can't ever get tired, Felicia?" We slid our way out and wiped the lint and dust off our pants. "I know of another hiding place. This one you might like."

Leading me downstairs, we entered her mother's room. "Are we supposed to be in here?"

"Chill out. My mother's got the overnight shift and Amanda's conked out on Valium."

"I think I should go," I said.

"Not *yet*," she implored. Her voice took on a childish whine—so different from the Elena Oyola who breezed past Ms. Mateo.

Elena slid open the door of a closet packed full with cardboard boxes, slacks, pants, and men's shirts on hangers. There were shined shoes and tattered sneakers, piles of the *Sports Illustrated* swimsuit issue and Charles Bronson videotapes, eight-tracks of Neil Diamond and Bread. Cracked 45s lined the carpeted closet floor. Sweatshirts preserved in plastic bags, razors, creams, green bottles of Brut, and sports socks.

"My mother can't get rid of it. Any of it. So she keeps him here, locked up in all the closets. I understand. I just wish we had more room for us. My father takes up so much space."

"Why are you showing me this?" I said.

"Amanda and I used to hide in here, wrap our faces with his shirts. We could still smell him if we concentrated hard enough.

If we breathed in deep enough. When I was eight, we spent a weekend in here," Elena laughed. "Of course, you know, we ate and went to the bathroom."

"I have to go," I said, my hand tight on the doorknob.

Elena lunged for me. "Let me color your hair."

"I like my color just fine."

That faraway look again. She stepped into the closet. "*Fine.* Shut the door on your way out."

OUR STATION WAGON barreled down the Brooklyn-Queens Expressway. My mother had told me we were going for a drive. No big deal. Avi weaved through traffic. We broke seventy. The heater didn't work, so we bundled up in layers of sweaters and draped blankets over our knees. Here in northern Valley Stream, instead of station wagons with the muffler dangling, scraping the concrete, the cars were sleek, foreign. We passed the high school, Elmont Memorial, with its electronic scoreboard and stadium-size football field, supermarkets with huge parking lots, Italian delis, strips of convenience and stationery stores. All the trees, so many of them that I lost count. Even barren, they cluttered the side-walks. Garbage bins were planted on the corner of every block, and I stuck my head out the window to scan the streets. I'd never seen any so clean.

"Roll up the window, Lisa, you're letting the heat out," my mother said.

"There is no heat," I said.

"Don't start with the smart mouth," she retorted.

"You see the cars? Follow them to the money, the big money," Avi said, a toothpick lodged between his teeth. We slowed down, drive-by style, gawking. "What did I tell you, Rosie? Didn't I tell you the money's here? We got to move on this, fast."

My mother scoped out the surroundings, the houses (where were the apartment buildings and fire escapes?), the streets free of subway stations and of buses spewing fumes. Although it was February, twinkling lights still decorated the windows; plastic re-enactments of the Annunciation filled the postage-stamp lawns. Everyone was *white,* or at least whiter than me.

"Are we moving?" I asked. "Here?"

"Maybe," my mother said, sipping Coke through a straw. "We just got here; it's too soon to tell."

Avi drove faster.

"Mom, everyone's *white.*"

My mother turned around. "What the hell do you think you are?"

I wanted to say "Not like them," but instead, I said, "It's too quiet here."

"Maybe that's what we need."

"No one knows us here," Avi said, driving down Merrick Road. "They sure like their diners."

Kids walked in pairs, sporting kelly-green-and-white letter jackets. Everyone matched so perfectly, unlike in Brooklyn, where you wore what you had, what your mother laid out for you in the morning, what the family could afford. We didn't carry pock-etbooks; we slung backpacks over one shoulder. But here, girls looked *girly,* softened and pretty, not like us with our red mouths and slicked-back hair.

"Are these the rich people?" I asked.

"In a way," my mother said. "Definitely richer than us. You have to drive farther out for the *real* money. Cold Spring Harbor, Oyster Bay, or out east, places by the water."

In the parking lot of Burger King, we shared fries, bacon cheeseburgers, onion rings, and packets of ketchup, then licked the grease from our fingers.

"Just wait," Avi said. "If your mother gets that job at Belmont, we'll be eating out every night at those fancy diners." The engine hummed.

Job, what job? What's going on? I wiggled in my seat. A bit of bacon lodged in my mouth.

"There's no job yet," my mother said dismissively.

The tension between them thickened, announcing itself.

"We need this, Rosie," he said. "We need to get clean. *George* . . ."

"I know," she hissed. "Do you always have to remind me?"

"LET ME SHOW you this trick," Elena said one evening in March. I suspected Amanda was home, but who knew. We sat on the carpet. Elena's mother had switched shifts with another nurse so she could be home to take care of Elena's sister during the day. What that entailed, Elena never told me.

With two fingers on either side of her throat, Elena pressed down hard, blocking her breath. I'd seen this before. There had been others. People not playing pretend. And I wondered why people felt comfortable dying in front of me, as if they were soothed by the idea that my face would be the last one they'd see. After a few moments Elena's eyes rolled upward and she fainted. She was out cold for a few minutes. The house was quiet. I shook her so violently that her hair whipped her face. I tried calling out to her crazy sister upstairs, who may not have even been crazy for all I knew, but Elena's fainting muted me. When she came to and her eyes fluttered open, she smiled at me.

"Scared you, didn't I? My father choked like that on a machine. In the hospital. They should have been more careful; they should have monitored and calibrated the equipment. They should have known. Now you see what I see. We're sisters now. Amanda, come closer."

My teeth chattered. I hated her. Marisol's face kept appearing to me, liverish, and I closed my eyes and opened them, seeing Elena's and my aunt's faces eclipsing each other. I remembered one night when we were staying at Marisol's, after my mother had left Eddie. We came home to find Marisol passed out; she had vomited on her clothes. My mother was quiet; she picked her sister up, held up her limp body in the shower, put her to bed. My mother put socks on Marisol's feet because, she said, she knew Marisol was afraid, since childhood, to sleep without them.

"You're insane," I said. I left Elena sprawled on her stairs. Left the front door wide open.

IN THE BATHROOM Ivy washed her hands. I edged closer. Although she tried hard to ignore me, I knew she couldn't resist.

"I heard you dissed the princess," she said.

"How did you . . . ?"

"Everyone knows. Now you want back in, right?"

"You were right," I said.

"About what?"

Next to her, in front of the mirror, I pulled off the rubber bands. I unraveled both of my braids. Ivy was silent, curious. The bands were tight, unyielding, and I struggled, but I would do this. I would let my hair out.

Ivy stepped closer and combed me out. "It ain't even that serious," she said. "I seen worse. 'Tima's sister— *birds* get lost in that shit. She be turning over in her sleep and pigeons be trying to jet out the window."

"I hate it," I said.

"I don't know, I think it's cool," she said. "At least it won't be like the princess. With all that shit she puts in her hair, it's going to fall out. Now, *that* would be some crazy shit to see. Flea, at least you won't go bald."

"I definitely don't have to worry about that." I laughed. "Ivy, I'm sorry."

"Don't even do it, girl. Don't be getting all emotional. Only one person can do the tears in this friendship."

When the bell rang and girls filed into the bathroom, toilets flushing, lipsticks uncapped, I wrapped my hair up in a bun.

"One day," Ivy said softly, "you should wear it out. For you, you know?"

"WE DON'T BELONG HERE," I said, walking down Law Street toward our new home, a basement apartment in a two-family house in a town called Valley Stream.

"We should have a parking space," my mother said, ignoring me. "We *are* paying $750 a month." She scanned the block for Avi's car. Had he found a space yet for that miniature house he deemed a vehicle, all the buckets of paint and rollers and trays crowding the backseat?

Trees lined the street, buds blooming and fragrant; sprinkler systems showered fertile lawns. People washed their cars outside, squeezed sponges into buckets, hosed chrome rims while blasting classic rock from their stereos. Girls wore tight jeans and pink shirts; Benetton bags swung from their wrists. I imagined they vacationed in shopping malls. On the way here, we drove past Green Acres Mall, where Alexander's and A&S towered, nothing like the cheap boutiques and mark-down stores on Fourth Avenue, where everyone was always going out of business.

In front of my new home, I peered at the pavement under my feet. I didn't want the bagel shops on every corner when there was Sunset Park and the sixteen-foot pool; I had vowed again to cross to the other side this summer.

Avi parked the station wagon, the front wheel up on the curb. Was I paranoid or did people glare, their double-dutch ropes freezing in midair?

"We don't belong here," I repeated.

"Who says?" my mother replied, rattling our set of keys. We

entered our new home through a side entrance. I'd never lived in a house before.

Inside, my mother and Avi prospected possibilities. The apartment was a junior one-bedroom with all-new appliances, beech cupboards, and a gleaming fridge. The eat-in kitchen had a large counter and several wooden stools.

"I could build a wall here," Avi said, gesturing to the middle of the living room, which would become, in part, my bedroom. In Brooklyn, I had my own room with two windows and a fire escape where I could watch squirrels rummaging through the trees. Light shimmering on the leaves, a yard filled with soil and mulch down below. My own forest. But in Valley Stream, Long Island, I would live in the dark, below ground level, sharing my room with a sofa and a television.

My mother clapped her hands, gushing. "Would you look at the carpet? Wall to wall!"

Carpet got me thinking about Elena and her dead father sealed up in her closet, and I swallowed hard. "Our apartment at home is bigger," I said.

"Lisa, soon this will be home," she said. "I can't believe how people here keep their doors unlocked, keys in the car. Everything so . . . *safe*. You'd never see this in Brooklyn."

"But my friends . . ."

"You'll make new ones," my mother said.

"Not like 'Tima or Ivy. I don't know this place or anyone here. Mom, we don't look like anyone here."

"We'll buy you some new clothes, dress like them, fit in. Soon you'll forget those people, you'll see."

"I don't want to leave," I said. As if it was that easy. Buy some new clothes, pin back the hair, and suddenly I'm a cheerleader waving a megaphone. But my mother understood none of this: how my voice took on a Spanish lilt; how in Brooklyn we learned to be tough, play with the boys, while it seemed that all girls here were bred to be prom queens and mall rats.

"Lisa, you're working my last nerve."

"It's not your choice," Avi said, snorting Afrin.

"You're not my father," I said.

"Thank God," he muttered.

"You want to end up like pregnant Anna, or locked up in the crazy house like Violet? Or maybe you want to be strung out, fucked up, like all the junkies on Ninth Avenue. You want to take after Honey, that addict who lived in Eddie's building, trading pussy for crack? Is that what you want? Because if we stay there, that's how you'll end up—pregnant, in jail, or dead."

I shook my head. "What I want is to go to Midwood. I want to go to school with my friends. I want to write."

"Write what?" Avi asked, puzzled. "Rosie, what does she write?"

"Lisa, I'm going to say this only once. We are moving here, to Valley Stream, to this house, in one month. This conversation is over."

Finally I felt accepted, I fit in, and now we were moving to this foreign island. But my mother saw none of this, the possibility that I might not be happy. All she could see were the lawns, the smooth, paved roads, and all the money.

Atlantic City
BROOKLYN 1988

IT WAS WINTER BREAK in seventh grade and we ushered in the holidays with chips, Wayne Newton, and hotel towels. We frequently took trips to Atlantic City in hopes of striking it rich. This year, on the way to the casino, Avi casually mentioned that he had a wife and three children. My mother had been filing her nails. Tossing the emery board out the window, she clawed the steering wheel with one hand, veering the car to the right. In the backseat, I held my breath; we were inches away from crashing into another car. Avi grabbed the wheel, pulled us over to the shoulder.

"You crazy? You want to get us killed?" Avi shouted.

"How could you fucking be *married*?" my mother said. "*We're* married."

"This is a road," Avi said. "There are other cars."

"Lisa, get out of the car. Avi and I have to talk," she said.

"She's not getting out of the car, Rosina, we're on a fucking *highway*."

My mother turned around and glared. "Don't make me ask you twice."

I got out of the car. The windows were rolled down to let out the smoke, so I could still hear them arguing.

The sides of the roadway were a ticker tape of black ice. Snow weighed down the mottled branches of rotten trees; birds flecked the ashen sky. Winter had a way of making everything appear sickly. Cars sped by, a blur of reds, blues, and blacks. I leaned on the car door, knees knocking; I balled my hands up inside my sleeves, the fake rabbit one my mother made me wear.

"And you're telling me this now?" my mother asked.

I wondered why my mother kept getting involved with men who belonged to other women. Eddie, Avi: These were men who had their own children and first wives; it seemed that they preferred my mother's body for everything but bearing their children.

"At least I'm telling you," Avi said.

"*After* we got married." The lighter quivered in my mother's hand; she could barely light her cigarette. "You didn't think I could use this information *before* we got married?"

"Calm down. Would you calm down," Avi said. He explained how he had fled the Israeli army on account of some sinus condition he'd self-diagnosed; he was a coward, not made for war. He left his family in Tel Aviv to emigrate here, and after a year, once he had settled and made a home for them, they would join him. "But then I met you," he said. "I wasn't supposed to meet you. That wasn't part of the plan."

"My heart fucking bleeds," she said. "In America, we believe in having one wife."

"I do have one wife here," Avi said. "You."

"You find this funny?"

"I'm not laughing."

"How long have you been married?" my mother asked.

Avi bowed his head. I saw him gripping the steering wheel with his hands.

"How *long*, Avi?"

"Fifteen years."

My mother got out and slammed the door.

"Another fucking wife, kids, a whole other *life*. I went through this once; I'm not going through it again. I'm not your backup pussy."

"Backup pussy? Why do you have to say that?"

"Tell me what this woman, your wife, knows about me."

Sighing, Avi said, "She doesn't. She still thinks I don't have enough money to bring them over."

"Unbelievable," my mother said. "You men never change."

"Never change?" Avi poked his head out the passenger-side window, cursing in Hebrew. "Do I hit you? Do I touch your daughter the way he did?"

I SAW GLASS BEADS colliding, damp, blue sheets, Eddie's legs spread wide. I wore the pink pajamas he bought me; everything in that house belonged to him. "Pretty girls should sleep warm," Eddie said. "Come under the covers with me, get in deep." He always had things I wanted between his legs: new clothes, toys, dinner. On one of our trips to New Jersey, my calves dangled out of the car, my skirt flew up above my waist. Eddie watched me from the mirror, stared at me through his aviator glasses until my mother massaged the back of his neck, told him to keep his eyes on the road. "Get your damn legs out of the window," my mother hissed from the front seat. The car had been swerving. That night my mother whispered that nothing with Eddie had ever happened. She told me that I dreamed my arm in a sling, my panties she found tangled in their sheets, the blood spots on the pillow. "It's not possible," she said, "you were always with me."

"But that was after I told you," I said, confused. My mother tucked me in tight, too tight, and she leaned over and said that nothing happened.

"It would be just like you to fuck this up for me," my mother said.

"I'M GOOD TO you both," Avi said, yelling out the car window. "Don't compare me to him."

I asked my mother if I could get back in the car, to which she responded, "You're choosing him? Get in, then. Be with him."

When I didn't move, my mother hissed, *"Go!"*

"Get in the car, Rosie," Avi pleaded.

"So is this what you do with all your money? Send it to them — that other family?"

Avi's eyes narrowed. "You know what we do with our money."

Time passed. My mother smoothed back flyaways, tamed her hair with her hands. It had gotten colder inside and out. "You're divorcing her," my mother said. It wasn't a question.

"I'm leaving her."

GAMBLERS ALWAYS GET the best rooms, the honeymoon or players' suites: red satin quilts, down-filled pillows, a bottle of a champagne chilled in a bucket by the window; we were treated like royalty. My mother and Avi would sleep on the sprawling mattress and I on the foldout couch. We'd been in the room for less than ten minutes when Avi raced down to the tables. But what about lunch? What about all the shops and lounge singers clad in sequins?

"He has to earn the room," my mother said.

"But I thought this was all free," I said.

"A long time ago so did I."

We showered and cocooned our hair with plush towels, which would be smuggled in our suitcases and duffle bags when we left. From the bathroom floor I watched my mother ease her body into a white silk dress. She rubbed cocoa butter on her legs, up her thighs. It was humid in the bathroom, the mirrors fogged, the air misting. My mother came into the bathroom to put on her earrings, two fat pearls. When she was done lathering foundation, she turned to me, pressed down on my earlobes. "They're closing up," she warned.

"I don't have any earrings," I said.

"What about the gold studs?" she asked.

"I lost them," I said. A few months ago, my mother had pawned them.

She took off her pearls, put them in my ears. Heavy, they weighed on my lobes. I was naked except for a bathrobe and my mother's earrings.

"Better," she said, as her thumb grazed my cheek, "much better."

"You're going to the tables," I said.

"The slots," she said, now in the other room. "Then Avi and I are going to have a little talk."

"How long will you be gone?"

"You have cable. Order room service, movies. But don't go overboard."

"Can I come with you?" I asked.

My mother paused, considered, but finally she said, "You're too young." Then she grabbed her pocketbook and left me in the red room.

I watched porn. In *New York City Woman*, John "Johnny Wad" Holmes plays a jaded Californian. Dissatisfied with orgies and gangbangs, he heads to New York seeking the perfect score. In the city, Holmes takes many jobs, as a caterer, a cab driver, and a playboy, until he finds his calling and poses as a doctor, an oral surgeon. Next to the operating table stands Holmes, clothed in a serene blue cotton surgical gown, being serviced by a bevy of peroxide blonds. We cut to a scene of John narrating his memoirs into a microphone and tape recorder. For the greater part of the movie, I had no idea what anyone was saying, what any of this meant, because there was only scene after scene of sex and I couldn't imagine doctors going at it like that. And then they were all coming at me: John in a stethoscope and a surgical cap, Mimi in sunglasses, and the nurses clutching clipboards; eyes unblinking, they followed him into the intensive care unit. Finally Holmes met his match with the affected rich girl, who, before the porn king, made inventive use of a champagne bottle between her legs.

I was fascinated but confused. My mother always acted as if sex was something to be feared; it caused disease and pregnancy. But the people in the movie didn't seem miserable; in fact, they always appeared happy. Yelping, groaning, laughing, and spraying the walls with expensive champagne, these were not sad, pregnant people. They were doctors and socialites living lives. Sexless, we were the miserable lot. It had become rare for me to hear Avi and my mother go at it; their room, once a hot sauna, had morphed into a cold space of four walls, a ceiling, and a floor, that contained their desperate murmurings, their bickering, for they fought constantly over their vials, *no dipping,* and how they would get more. I fell asleep with the television on.

Later that night, the door flung open.

"Your hands aren't clean," my mother slurred.

"They're clean enough," Avi said.

They giggled and stumbled about the room like children, dropping things, knocking lamps over. Avi tried to quiet my mother, claiming that I could wake up any minute, and my mother dismissed him. "She sleeps through everything."

It was then they noticed the movie and Avi said, "We have this one."

"Did she order this?"

"She must have gotten it by mistake," Avi said. "It doesn't matter, she doesn't know what it means."

"She's *twelve*, not five," my mother said, momentarily concerned.

With one eye open, I saw Avi gesture at the television with one hand and slide the other up under her dress. "We could do that," he said.

I was forgotten.

Avi scattered so many chips and bills on the bed, they fell like leaves. Apparently they had won big.

"Take that gold off your finger," Avi said, "Tomorrow I buy you diamonds."

"Did you buy her diamonds? Your little Israeli wife."

"I buy diamonds for only you," he said, and they tumbled onto the bed. Their bodies knotted, and after a few moments I could hear my mother moaning; her hands clawing at Avi's back, they clung together like little crabs. Years later my mother would tell me that she never particularly enjoyed sex with anyone, especially Avi; rather, she merely saw it as a means to get what she wanted. A body bartered, eager to manipulate. Men, my mother told me, like women who fuck like whores.

I spent the next day abandoned in the hotel room. Our trips were always like this. Ignored during the day, brought out for dinner. The last time we had been here, we stayed in the Egyptian suite, where everything was gold, even the curtains; our closet was a brass sarcophagus, and two gold-plastered lions in sphinx pose greeted us in the bathroom. That time I was an archaeologist, rummaging the room for jewels, the closets for mummies, whose brains, I learned in school, were yanked through their noses with a metal hook. I cranked up the thermostat, got the room nice and hot to a point where I thought I'd faint.

Sometimes it was better to live in my head.

Before dinner, my mother coated my hair with Vaseline. I sat on the toilet seat while she sectioned my thick hair and parted it down the middle as I tried to wiggle free.

"What?" she asked. "What's wrong with you?"

"I don't want to wear it like that anymore," I said.

"You look pretty like this."

"I look like I'm four."

My mother kept braiding my hair in the damn pigtails. A cigarette was clamped between her lips. Her hands were nimble, working quickly, weaving my hair. Controlling it. "So much work, this hair," she said.

I wondered why she had to make me feel like I was always a chore, an obligation that needed tending. "I don't want the braids, mom," I said.

Avi stood at the doorway, his belly spilling over his trousers. "Let's go," he said.

My hair was unfinished when my mother stood back. "All this time I spent on you. You ungrateful little girl."

"Don't start, Rosie," Avi said. "I'm starving."

"We'll get your fucking steak," she said. Shoving him aside, she sat on the bed, buckled her shoes. She waltzed in and out of the bathroom, primping, taking care of herself, while I held my hair in my hands. Here was my mother's famous silent treatment: She was disciplined; she could ignore you for weeks if she wanted to. Tears, pleas, nothing could break this woman. She alone would decide when you were worthy of being spoken to again.

I pulled my hair up in a bun, just like hers. My mother opened the window, smoked outside of it.

Avi sat on the navy and gold–upholstered chair, hands on his knees. "Are we going?" he called to her.

"We're going."

As my mother walked past me, she narrowed her eyes and said, "*You* will not be having steak."

What had been the grave assault against her? I couldn't pinpoint what, exactly, I had done this time to upset her. I looked at my shoes; I would not cry in front of her. Avi unfolded his hands, got up from the chair and moved toward the door. She charged after; he held open the door, allowed her to pass him.

We followed her down the stairs.

AFTER DINNER, YOU couldn't pry Avi away from the tables. You could be dead, lying on the floor, and he'd merely step over you to get a prime seat at the players' table. The world had been reduced to black and red chips and a patch of green cloth. Avi called the dealers by their first names. Some called him Avi; the real players called him Slick. Behind his back the Russians called him the Dirty Jew because he always took their money. *Look at the curls,* they said, *look at the nigger skin.* Avi was only mildly Jewish to me, which is to say in comparison to the Hassids who donned black wool coats and hats year-round, observing Shabbat while Avi watched Dallas, who turned up their noses at Avi, at his dark skin. When I asked Avi about this, he chewed on his toothpick and spat at the ground. "Sons of bitches," he called them: "No one is a Jew to them but them. Half of them have never seen my country. They go once in a lifetime, call it their pilgrimage."

My mother and I left him and headed into the cocktail lounge.

Four hours later, Avi found us. He hunched low in our booth. You could practically see suitcases hanging from his eyes. His lips were dry, chapped. "It's all gone," he said.

"Tell me something I don't know," my mother said.

"I don't know what happened."

"I do. You lost all of our money, *again*. Five thousand dollars down the goddamn toilet. You fucking *waste*."

Glaring at her, Avi said, "Don't start. I don't want to hear it."

"I told you to stop. I told you to quit while you were ahead. We should have gone home like I said. But *no*, you had to stay here, you had to play the big shot, win *all* the money. Look where that got you."

"I was winning," Avi said, confused. "I was so up; I don't understand how I lost my game."

"I hope you at least have money for gas, or will I have to pay for that, too?"

"Goddamn, woman, can't you just let it go?"

"Four fucking hours I waited. Tell me, big shot, where are my

THE SKY ISN'T VISIBLE FROM HERE

diamonds now? Look at you," she spat, "you can't even control yourself."

Avi laughed so hard he started coughing. "And you know all about *control*."

"Go fuck yourself," she said.

"I already did," he said. "Three years ago when I married you."

I gasped. She would kill Avi. My mother would bludgeon him right here, in front of everyone, with our plates, stab him with our forks and steak knives.

She rose, calm, pushing her cocktail glass to one side. "I'm going to let that little comment slide on account of the fact that you probably feel guilty for gambling all of our holiday money away. You must feel like the little man that you are." To me, she said, "Come, Lisa, we're going."

I gulped down my cola. You had to act fast around my mother because you never knew when you'd be leaving.

"Your wife can have you," she said. "You're worthless to me."

My mother dragged me by the arm, and when I turned around, Avi appeared small, weary; a broken man with his head in his hands. Perhaps he would have been better off in Israel, in the army, instead of here, fighting a war he would never win.

Stop-Times

PORTLAND, OREGON

2005

WE'RE CHILDREN NOW, running in the wet grass. We could be four or ten. But really we're adults, thirty or thirty-five years old, and authors, running amok at a Portland writing conference. The girl who writes fairy tales lets down her hair and calls us out to the lawn. I envy her those flimsy curls, so loose and bouncing. Forget it all. Be wild in a new way, be un-me. But back to the game. We all debate the rules of freeze tag. Tossing down aluminum chairs, dodging tables covered in red cloth — so much red, I think, for a table, for outside, for the verdant field — we're giddy, delirious. It's summer; the sun warms me. We make new rules, because that's what children do, create worlds that adults find ways to ruin. We determine that the concrete is our safe place. A boy, fixated on blinding bees and secret passageways within trees, constructs a fortress with a candy-striped hula hoop. He used to be a drinker and a junkie. *It's safe in here,* he says. Another boy rolls up his long blue sleeves, revealing stories written on his arms. So we run, we sprint; we lose our breath and catch it again. I think of my mother briefly, and the dreams I used to have about her and children who would follow her, running blindly through grass. I'm an adult now and it feels good to run, to know that this is all real. We call for stoptimes. We go barefoot, we freeze, and our pants might be grass stained, who's to tell. Leave that work for the adults. We want to go back, start over, be children again. A girl clutches her broken shoe, her neck ornamented with beads and wood, calls out, *I'll trade my mother for yours.* We laugh. I examine my nails, and although they are lacquered, they are chipped and dirty—children's nails. *The boys,* a sweet girl from Northampton warns, *are always faster.* And I imagine we could be like this all day long, forever if we wanted to, feet padding, arms flapping, preparing for flight. Until we are reprimanded: the tables are dangerous, the chairs hazardous. *Some of the adults, the older ones, would prefer you move to the other field. Why not play it safe,* says an adviser with those eyebrows all weedy and wild in a way that unnerves me. *Move on to the other green. A clearing.* Reminding us, but kindly, that we are not children.

It's almost cocktail hour, the adviser (we snicker, call him the warden) offers. He points to a dining area inside filled with bowls of crushed ice and bottles of white and red wine. We hear a shaker shaking.

We're done with drinking hours, I say. A third glass of wine isn't my life anymore; I'm on a two-drink maximum. I look forward to early risings free from hangover.

How about sober hour? the boy chides, hula hooping. He's good at that, I think, the hooping. In another life, he drank more than I did, if you could believe. He knocked them back, swallowed them down, and went one for one, until he saw black. We swap stories like baseball cards. We laugh because our stories always start like this: *That one night when I was drunk, that other night when I was high.* And they always end like this: *The rest I don't remember.*

The girl with the flounce says, *I think I like that. Let's boycott the hour.*

Stop-time, the girl from Northampton shouts.

The children have spoken.

Before Cocaine
BROOKLYN 1984

WE WERE HAPPIEST standing on our hands in the sand, feet to the stars. My mother and I packed our towels, along with our matching sunglasses with the white plastic trim, my electric-blue beach pail. We were ready to comb the sand for shells, hit the water for a cool swim. And that Sunday, in 1984, before cocaine, we took a trip to Coney Island, boarded the subway to the southernmost point of Brooklyn. The whole ride I stared out the window as we sailed above ground, waiting for the first glimpse of the shore and the seagulls that swarmed the nearby station stops, ravaging trash cans for orange rinds and rotten candied apples. We were running away! Hot dogs, cheese fries that burned the roofs of our mouths and left us to click our tongues at the stringy skin, the bombastic music and glittering bikinis—we were leaving our somber Boro Park apartment with its pale light and barren cabinets. Free, we let the shackles fall from our ankles like loose bracelets.

My mother strutted down the boardwalk in her frayed jean shorts. She didn't believe in bras or any material fashioned with wire, so brown nipples poked against her peasant blouse. We shared the corpselike pallor, the similar pearl skin that would never tan, would only burn. I was always embarrassed about baring skin, but my mother paraded around in skimpy shorts, cropped tops, legs and armpits unshaven. To strangers we must have looked under-exposed, like an X-ray.

We were hungry. My mother cut in at the snaking line at Nathan's Famous, and a woman hissed in disbelief, sucked her teeth until my mother turned around and scowled. "You talking to me?"

This woman was all pockmarked, loose skin, with a face full of smoke. Her coarse hair was set with pink plastic rollers, secured with a thick hairnet. I remembered the previous summer, when we lived with Eddie, when we sat on the stoop on Ninth Avenue, my mother taunting all the women who dared to leave their houses without their hair *done*. Thick hair coiled up in a bun with a lone roller for the bangs; hairnets and shower caps covering a wet scalp—these would send my mother reeling. She thought it a disgrace and she'd let you know it. "Excuse me, are we in your home? Is this stoop your goddamn couch? Pull a comb through that shit!" Obsessive, my mother guarded her scalp, checked in various mirrors she kept in her smock, pocketbook, and leather coat, paranoid about flyaways, a single strand out of its place. She never dared to leave the house otherwise. And unlike the women who fixed their daughters' hair in public, yanking at kinky curls, plaiting tight ringlets, my mother braided my thick, unruly mane in the privacy of our bathroom.

The woman at Nathan's Famous rolled her head. Pursing her lips, she made a *pssst* sound and mumbled to her friend in Spanish while my mother stood on line, defiant. Arms folded into her chest, my mother stared her down, ready to pounce. The woman shifted uncomfortably from foot to foot and finally looked away.

At the counter I ordered for us: two cheeseburgers, fries, and two large Cokes. We sat on a picnic bench and fed each other soggy fries swathed in ketchup and cheddar cheese.

"Did you see the look on that woman's face?"

"You got her good," I said, munching on my burger. Every so often I glanced over my shoulder to make sure we were safe.

"They think they can get over on us because we're white, but never be afraid to step up," my mother said. "You have to be fearless, never let yourself be vulnerable, never cry. Once they see weakness—" my mother snapped her fingers, "—forget it."

I nodded. I had no idea what my mother meant by any of this, but back then I never thought to question her logic, I took what she said for gospel, because this was my mother. She was always right.

Gathering a handful of fries, my mother said, "I'm not afraid of anyone." She shoveled food in her mouth while studying me, arching her brows, nodding knowingly, but all this was lost on me, for I was a nine year old who longed for the carousel bejeweled with iridescent mirrors and glinting lights, with seats that swung round, or the pirate ship that soared high in the air and rocked back down. My heart paused.

"Take me on the rides," I said.

All the rides in Coney Island have a height requirement, and a flat palm halted us at each ticket booth. But with a quick glare from my mother, we were ushered past the chain ropes and we hopped on the pirate ship shaped like a giant canoe. She buckled me in, yanked on the strap, hard. I felt secure. A man in white shorts and matching polo top walked around and elevated a bar lock that jutted up into my stomach, and my mother said, "We're safe now." And it was always when we were about to embark on a ride that my mother would repeat the story about her friend who was trapped upside down on the Cyclone for forty-five minutes, her red wig falling, then caught, dangling from a steel beam.

As the operator pulled on a lever and we began to slowly rock, I cried, "Jesus, mom!"

"What?"

"Do you always have to?" I asked in my most adult voice but then stopped myself when I realized that I sounded exactly like my mother.

"It's just a *story*," she snapped, "it's not *real*."

I glanced at her, puzzled, and she responded by shaking her head, clucking her tongue. "Let's just try to enjoy the ride," she said.

After a few moments it was as if nothing had happened, and we clutched each other's hands as the boat began to swing faster. I loved this thrill—the stomach drop, the quick, stolen breaths, the momentary fear that the ride would never stop, we could fall, and the ground would give way. We were wild-eyed; raising our arms, we screamed when the boat crashed down from the air. I imagined my mother and me drowning. As a child, I orchestrated grand deaths—holocausts and catastrophes—and how we'd survive them. Airplanes plummeting from the sky, breaking the ocean's surface, and somehow we'd emerge from the wreckage. I reveled in these fantasies and daydreamed about them in painstaking detail, down to the outfits we wore and evening news telecasts. So here I was on an amusement-park ride, picturing the rods and beams collapsing and caving in, my mother and I being flung into the ocean. Breaking through the water, fighting the undertow, we'd swim our way to shore. Accessing death made life more real.

But then we ascended, raising our feet as high as we could. The sky was this close. And I screamed until there was no more voice, until the wind was the loudest whisper.

Coming off the ship, my legs wobbled and I felt nauseous. When I ran to the nearest garbage can, my mother held my hair back as I tossed my lunch. Massaging my neck, she asked if I was okay, if I wanted to go home.

"I want to be here," I said. I wanted to go to the beach and into the water, to come back later for the carousel and Ferris wheel. But first the haunted house. Today there would be time for everything.

We entered the House of Horrors. Inside, it was dark and smelled of mothballs, of clothes left too long in closets. Torches went aflame in the caverns, illuminating bug-eyed owls hooting, wolves howling. Mist swelled; rising from the floor, it seeped into our car as we inched along on the tracks. A scarecrow clutching a hatchet lurched out. Skeletons danced, ghouls waved scythes. For an adult these images and their stiff, marionette movements would have been comic, but back then in the pitch black, when I couldn't see my hand in front of my face, I screamed. My mother held me for the entire ride. "Don't you know," she said, "that no one could ever hurt us?"

After, we walked around for a bit and my mother bought me a Coke from a hot dog vendor on the boardwalk. I took small, measured sips.

"Race you!" she said, and we sprinted to the beach. We collapsed a few feet from the shoreline, and my mother tossed her red towel onto the sand. "Look at how big you are. I remember when you were this tall," she said, and lowered her hand to her knees. "One day, you'll be even bigger than me. Imagine that."

"I'm fat." Gesturing at my jean shorts, which threatened to burst at the seams, plump thighs squeezing out, I said, "I'm the only kid that shops in the juniors section."

"Not fat, *healthy*. You come from me and you're beautiful. Don't forget it."

"Maybe I shouldn't eat so much," I said to myself, but abandoning packages of Little Debbie chocolate snack cakes, jumbo cheeseburgers, and titan-size bags of Cheese Doodles was unimaginable. What else would I eat? I eyed my mother's gangly legs with envy and fumed that she managed to stay so lean.

My mother kept repeating that all this fat talk was nonsense, that it was all in my head, but when she realized that none of what she said registered, she gave up and said, "Let's go in the water."

"You go. I'll watch our stuff." From my book bag I unearthed several paperbacks from the Sweet Valley High series as well as a new series, Pearls. I didn't care for Nancy Drew or any of the smart, precocious girls whose quick wits and trusty pets saved the day. Instead I opted for sororities and rich teenagers who wore their sun-kissed hair in high ponytails, donned pearls, and drove Fiats with vanity plates. I devoured these novels about haughty, beautiful girls and the boyfriends who loved them, for I was desperate for access to this exclusive clique that offered endless fun and weekends with the top down. Girls in Sweet Valley never got jumped in grade school because they were white and unpopular. God forbid they should soil their figures with Burger King battered onion rings and Little Debbie snack cakes. The Pearl girls had credit cards and coming out parties, and although I didn't know what these things meant, I wanted them.

We took off our sandals and shook out sand and rock. Digging my big toe into the sand, I howled from the scalding temperature. I rested my feet on my beach towel while my mother applied baby oil to her legs. She took the sun like sacrament.

My mother never learned how to swim; the rollicking water frightened her. She feared unseen things—jellyfish, suckerfish, molten rock, and glass. No, she would venture in but stay close to shore where it was safe.

She approached the water with caution. She roved for seashells and colored glass; she adored these pretty souvenirs and filled glass vases and jars with amber shards and baby conches. Entering the water, treading until she was waist deep, she dog-paddled, slapped the foamy waves with her hands. My mother made certain that she was surrounded by children floating on inflatable rafts, that lifeguards were nearby. After ten minutes, she paddled back to shore.

She wrung out her hair. Foam lapped her ankles and washed her shells out into the ocean. A strip of sun, a ticker tape of light encased her in gold, made her mythic, rendering an impression of her strange kind of beauty—soft but annihilating. As she journeyed toward me, her stomach glistened with goose bumps. I closed my book. Above me, her hair dripped onto Jessica Wakefield's face.

"Always reading, you. We're here to relax, have fun!" she said, sealing my book shut.

"I *am* having fun," I said, but headed toward the water then.

When I was five, I had taught myself how to swim. The kiddie pool at Sunset Park was four feet deep, and my mother held me up while I trod water. When I grew confident, I broke away from her, swimming, snorting chlorine up my nose. On our way home that day, I had felt my mother's jealousy, her voice seared by envy. She was twenty-five and water scared her and here was her daughter, unafraid and swimming.

The water buoyed me up like a mattress; my stomach surfed wave crests. The tide sucked me out farther from shore. I swam past the floating orange safety cones and thin ropes, with my neck stiffly holding my head up, as if I were on the lookout. Arching my back, I pressed on, raising each arm to stroke the water down and back. When I swam as far as I could, I flipped onto my back and rested on the waves. Barely paddling my arms beside my hips, I made the smallest of movements to allow me to stay afloat. I was so small, I wondered if anyone could see me.

From a distance, my mother was a luminous silhouette waving her arms in the air, motioning for me to return. I charged back.

"Are you fucking crazy? You could have gotten yourself killed out there!" she shouted, as I settled onto the sand. My chest was heaving. Nearby families turned around and stared. I looked at the boy who tripped and collapsed into the sand castle that he'd spent all day building, an estate reduced to rubble. His face exploded into tears. Twin girls gyrated their thick hips to Spanish music that blared from a battery-operated tape deck, their nutmeg skin glistening. I focused my attention on everything but my mother.

"It wasn't that far out," I said, although I knew it really was.

"You need to be where I can see you." Her hands trembled and an unfamiliar look registered on her face — fear. "You want to give me a heart attack? You want me to lose my only child? Is that what you want?"

"I'm sorry," I said, drying my legs with a towel.

After she calmed down, she stared at me while I gathered up my things. I hated feeling her eyes on me like that, studying me. Smiling, she told me that I was a girl who knew no limits. Like mother, like daughter. And part of me wanted to tell her I was the one who could swim farther out and did — beyond the safe point — but instead I kept quiet. As we left the beach, my mother dragged her red towel along the sand.

"Don't ever scare me like that again," she said.

Dusk turned the saffron sky, vibrant with pink and orange, to a deep violet. The children waded in, bruised red by their hot sunburns, smelling of saltwater taffy behind the ears. Mothers rubbed Noxzema on the children's backs. Black water crested, dazzling liked a lost jeweled purse. On the footpath leading up to the train station, my mother and I feasted on boiled peanuts, licking the sweet honey off our fingers, and sipped pink lemonade from plastic cups. We quoted dialogue from a recent *Three's Company* episode and analyzed *General Hospital,* notably the Luke and Laura saga, in great detail. Would they get back together? These things were terribly important to us, and we spent a great deal of time picking apart the soap's story line.

On the train ride back, I curled up under her arm and rested there, feeling soothed by the humming of the subway, the steady rise and fall of her chest. Through the window, I could see the storm clouds swarming.

At Fort Hamilton Parkway, we got out and it was pouring. We ran down Forty-fourth Street with our beach pails and pillowcases filled with half-eaten candies, sand-encrusted sunglasses, and soggy towels.

My mother grabbed my hand and we fled across the two avenues to our apartment. She was faster, as always, and I trailed behind. Our clasped hands separated and I watched her skip ahead, giddy and wet. I held up my pail, collecting the rain. Every so often my mother looked back, made sure I was right behind her.

"You're this close," she said, sprinting.

As we entered our building, our cackles echoed throughout the hallway; we collapsed against the wall, laughing. Taking the stairs two at a time, we made our way into the apartment and peeled off our clothes right there in the kitchen. Naked, we stood facing each other, giggling.

My mother and I stayed up late that Sunday, feeding each other spare ribs and pork fried rice out of white take-out cartons, watching old movies. All talk of school or work was banished. And I closed my eyes, desperately wanting to tell my mother that I loved her, really loved her, but I felt that saying those small words might alter the easy fun we were having. I didn't know why, but I felt the mood might irrevocably shift, and I didn't want to do anything that would ruin a moment that I had only read about—two girls gossiping, watching TV, happy.

"You're mine," she kept saying, and it felt good to belong to someone.

"I'm yours," I sang back, beaming. "I'm yours."

Acknowledgments

I am humbled to have a fine publisher and home with Algonquin Books. I'm indebted to Amy Gash, my fearless, tireless editor, who, with her careful, critical eye, helped shape this manuscript from its most nascent form. Thank you, Amy, for consistently raising the bar and cracking the whip.

I am deeply grateful to have an agent who saw the potential in ten pages—thank you, Matthew Carnicelli, for your unwavering support.

Rebecca, you are one of the few people who helped me to go to the places I didn't want to go.

I couldn't have found a more beautiful friend in Susan Chi. Your friendship has changed me in ways I couldn't have imagined. Thank you for keeping me sane and for holding my hand—even when I didn't think it needed holding.

Cris Beam and Robin Goldman—warriors, titans. Without you both, I wouldn't have been courageous enough to embark on this journey.

To my friends, who are my family — my heart is deeply warmed by your friendship, laughter, and support. Thank you.

And thanks, Gus, *dad,* for always being by my side.